God's Method

Principles That Will
Propel You into Your Life
Calling

K.D. Johnson

Copyright © Katherine Duke Johnson
for KD Johnson Ministries & Marimae Publishing Co.
All Rights Reserved.

No part of this publication may be reproduced, stored in a retrieval system, or transmitted to any form or by any means – electronic, mechanical, digital, photocopy, recording, or any other, except for brief quotations in printed reviews, without the prior permission of the author. Please direct your inquiries to info.kdjohnson@gmail.com

Unless otherwise notated, scripture quotations are taken from the NASB - New American Standard Bible©1960, 1962, 1963, 1968, 1971, 1972, 1973, 1975, 1977, 1995 by the Lockman Foundation. Used by permission. (www.Lockman.org).

Duke-Johnson, Katherine (K.D.),
God's Method/Principles That Will Propel You Into Your Life Calling
ISBN:978-0692076729 (trade paper)
1. Biblical Studies. 2. Christian Living

Marimae Publishing
Charlotte, NC

Dedication

This book is dedicated to Mariah Faith. My first granddaughter who is so precious to me and gives me great joy. To every sister, be it leader, teacher, mentor, missionary, pastor, worship leader and encourager, who unselfishly imparts of the wealth that God has entrusted to you. I thank you for I know that I can because you do. To the Lord who has always opened the doors that should be opened to me and closed doors that should be shut. I am eternally grateful for my daughter, Meagan Ashley, who has been with me through thick and thin and to my husband, Kirk Lee for your continued love and support.

Endorsements

It is my pleasure to give an endorsement to a masterfully written book, "God's Method." Minister Kate Johnson, an anointed and equipped vessel, has written an excellent read which will be used as a tool for helping the saints of God to fulfil their purpose and walk out their destiny.

You will discover the rich life changing application of scripture and moreover, some examples on how to develop and find your place within the Body of Christ, which is so crucial in the world in which we live. You will also be inspired by the fresh approach of learning and applying God's truth to your everyday life.

Reverend Dr. Errick Redmond, Pastor
King's Church, Belmont, NC

***

I have had the pleasure of knowing this author for well over 25 years. She is a woman of strength, dedication, tenacity, and dedication. It is no surprise that she was inspired to write this amazing book.

One of the things most needed in the Christian community today is a reminder of how important it is that we solidify our walk with God and in so doing secure the necessary tools that will aid in us doing so. This book is one of those aides.

In this book, we are reminded of God's method for our success in fulfilling His divine will and purpose for our lives, which includes obedience and prayer. From a theological perspective, this book is clearly written and easy to understand. This book is a must read for all who fully believe that if you acknowledge Him in all your ways He will direct your path.

Rev. Beverly Caesar Sherrod, Associate Pastor
Bethel Gospel Tabernacle, Jamaica, NY

***

God's Method is a read filled with spiritual nuggets for the seasoned believer as well as for the new convert. Min. Kate explores the journey to victorious Christian living concisely and with freshness that draws you in and leaves you with a renewed perspective on what it means to live in the fullness of all that God has intended. You will enjoy reading this book.

Overseer Dorothy A. McGuire, Senior Pastor
Life Changing Church, Charlotte, NC

Table of Contents

Acknowledgments
Foreword
Introduction
Chapter 1: The Reality of Being Stuck in
    a Dry Place.. 9
Chapter 2: The Catalyst of Conversion................19
Chapter 3: The Framework of Faith...................29
Chapter 4: The Obligation of Obedience.............41
Chapter 5: The Persistence of Prayer..................49
Chapter 6: The Person of the Holy Spirit..............59
Chapter 7: The Fruit of the Spirit in Practice.........83
Chapter 8: The Fortitude of Fellowship 89
Chapter 9: The Propensity Towards Propulsion......99
Chapter 10: The Matter of the Heart..................109
Chapter 11: Conclusion: It All Depends on You....113
About the Author
Book List

Acknowledgments

Thank you to the many friends who have prayed for me to see this book brought to life. Overseer Dorothy McGuire for proofing the manuscript concerning the biblical text upon which the truths of these chapters were built. Thanks to Rev. Dr. Errick Redmond and the family of Kings Church. Special thanks to my mother, Lillian Duke for reading the rough draft of this book. Thank you to Harvest Outreach Center and KBC Nursing Home and Outreach Ministries for the opportunity to share in sermons much of what is contained in this book, and to the homeless and disenfranchised at our gatherings. To Rev. Beverly Caesar-Sherrod and Dr. Charles A. Barrett who believed in me and for lasting friendship. Last, but not least, thank you to every prayer warrior for times of refreshing and fellowship. Indeed, you have helped to strengthen my faith.

Foreword

It is my pleasure to offer a few introductory remarks for my friend's latest book, *God's Method*. Having known Katherine (Kathy) Duke-Johnson for more than 20 years, initially as a colleague in music ministry, I have always respected her commitment to God and His people. Whether through writing songs with powerful lyrics and melodies, leading congregations in worship and praise, or through the written word, Kathy has always been clear about her purpose: to help people experience God in a manner that is both real and relevant.

Having read *God's Method*, I am encouraged that this necessary element of effective 21st century ministry remains. Like any other book, including The Bible, knowledge of the author provides the reader with significant insight into its content. For this reason, I am grateful that Kathy has included personal experiences throughout the book to help illustrate various concepts.

She never intended to present herself as one who has already attained, but like the Apostle Paul, she, too, continues to press toward the mark of the higher calling of God, which is in Christ Jesus! In an era that discourages Christian leaders from sharing their humanity and imperfections so that we can grow together, *God's Method,* has been written by a true servant who is continually striving to become all that God has created her to be.

Among other things, *God's Method* is appropriate for Christians in any stage of spiritual maturity. If you are just beginning your personal relationship with Christ, be encouraged: there is something within these pages to help strengthen your faith in Christ. And even for those that have been walking and talking with The Lord for quite some time, the biblical principles are excellent reminders of the fundamentals of our faith.

Although, it is virtually impossible to completely, separate, any author from her work, Kathy provides scriptural support for her positions, along with concrete examples to help illustrate concepts. Such a combination is a powerful recipe to ultimately give readers the necessary tools to live more victoriously as Christians.

Although, *God's Method*, can be read in a single day, I would encourage you not to do this. Instead, consider reading a single chapter each day. Afterwards, set aside a few moments to intentionally meditate on its contents and allow The Lord to speak to you personally. In other words, ask him to show you what each chapter specifically means for your life? And after you ask Him, wait for His answer. I know that He will speak to you.

Charles A. Barrett, PhD
President, CAB Publishing Company, LLC
Co-Editor, "Gumbo for the Soul"

Introduction

Connectivity

God desires to be in unique connection with humankind. He is so desirous of intimate relationship and fellowship with us, that He provided a method, so that we can live in harmony and fellowship with Him.

There is no other creation that God has enacted this kind of plan. He formulated a method whereby; men's sins are erased, and we can live in the sanctuary of His presence. A symbol I use for this connectivity is the lightbulb. The lightbulb represents being connected to the ultimate power source--God. When we are connected to the power source, we are electrified by His power that manifests in the form of spiritual light in our lives that brightens and illuminates the place where it is stationed.

Light and energy in our homes does not just happen. There is a process by which electricity flows. Light is a form of energy. In short, energy flows through a thin glass tube, making the glass glow. Just as a lightbulb illuminates a room whereby we can see that which is around us; the Holy Spirit illuminates (glows in) our spirit man. This allows us to know Christ in an intimate way.

The lightbulb does not illuminate without fulfilling prescribed scientific steps and processes of bringing together its components: Wires, filament, fuse, cap, stem, gases and energy. These elements come together in succinct fashion to bring about

God's Method

the result of light. Separately, these elements are powerless. Brought together in a scientific order, they produce light.

Comparing this marvel to the Holy Spirit, God wants to bring about spiritual light in our hearts that electrifies the world and brings light to dark places. To be a useful and effective vessel for kingdom business, God has a succinct method by which he matures and makes us useful for His purpose.

What follows are spiritual elements brought together through a method of God's plan to change, empower and electrify our spirit man to be victorious and effective, for the cause of Christ on the earth. The result of this method will set us on the path to experience personal triumph in our daily walk.

In Chapter One, we discuss the reality, that many of us are and have been stuck in a dry place for many years. We believe, that God is a miraculous God, who wants to be intimately involved in the circumstances of our lives. Somehow, we have not been as effective in our walk as we could be. We discuss coming to terms with the realization that we need to move from this place.

In Chapter Two, we deal with the catalyst of conversion. We cannot change our world if we are takes pleasure in the worlds iniquity. The Bible says, that we should be in the world, but not of the world. We must first, be converted and undergo spiritual transformation as a first step to victory.

Chapter Three discusses the framework of faith being a primary necessity of getting God's attention. Many speak of faith as being simple, which has the connotation of being easy. We neglect talking about faith as a challenge and an act of courage. We rarely vocalize that faith can be hardest during a time of pain and/or trials. The testing of our faith is widely spoken of in the

New Testament. We need to understand that faith is not faith, unless it has been tested. Faith often involves a choice. What will I choose to do or say when faced with uncertainty and testing?

The obligation of obedience is discussed in Chapter Four. Discipleship begins with the confession of faith. Moving from there, we become His disciples. A disciple is one who submits to a teacher's tutelage and becomes a learner. As an apprentice learns from his teacher, he becomes acclimated to the trade, growing in skill and expertise. We too, must learn from the master teacher. We must follow His instructions, with complete obedience, to grow as overcomers in our spiritual walk.

Many of us agree, that prayer is foundational to the Christian life. Persistent prayer, which is the topic of the fifth chapter, is a practice which our success depends upon. The absence of prayer often results in our failure. The Bible talks about coming to God continually. Many believe that we should just ask God one time and that's it for a specific prayer request. If we pray about it again, we are told that we don't have faith.

To the contrary, the Bible talks about praying women and the example of Jacob pulling on the angel to bless him. This speaks of persistence in prayer and the ability to get God's attention on your behalf. It speaks to our attitude of being determined and desperate for God. How many of us are desperate for the presence of God and for Him to work on our behalf to the point where time doesn't matter in our pursuit for answers?

Further, persistent prayer gets the attention of Heaven. The Bible speaks of various people, who came to God for an answer to prayer. They came not once, not twice, but again and again. (Luke 18:1; Eph. 1:7)

God's Method

Sometimes it may be necessary to come to God several times before receiving an answer. Not because God is hard-of-hearing, but because, God is dealing with us in the process of prayer. Today's culture teaches us that faith is demonstrated when we pray about a situation once and no more. After we have prayed, we are to stand, decree and affirm. However, there are those instances where God wants us to come away with Him and get in a place of determination that we must hear from Him so he can change us and sometimes our expectation.

We would be remiss in not discussing the person of the Holy Spirit (Chapter Six). The Holy Spirit is the third person of the Trinity. We describe the Holy Spirit as a person and not as an *"it"* because *He* indeed has feelings. Ephesians 4:30 says, *"that we can grieve the Holy Spirit."* Hebrews 10 and 29 says, *"that the Holy Spirit can be insulted."* Ephesians 15 and 28 says, *"that the Holy Spirit thinks good things."*

We speak of the Holy Spirit, interceding on our behalf. As such, He was alive yesterday and He is alive today. He will live in the future. His personality is evident as He is involved in the affairs of man. He indwells the believer for victorious living. We discuss further in this chapter, God's desire for us to be filled with the person of the Holy Spirit. These components work together as a method, whereby man can be connected to God in an intimate way. Secondly, He is our aide to live victoriously in this life as effective witnesses that Jesus Christ is indeed alive and that the church has not lost its connectivity to the divine reality of God's love for humanity. We may have lost some footing along the way and our testimonies may be bruised, but God by His Holy

Spirit draws us back into fellowship with Him in these end times and His character remains the same.

The Fruit of the Spirit is discussed in Chapter Seven. Delineated in Galatians the 5th chapter is the fruit of love, joy, peace, patience, kindness, goodness, faithfulness and self-control. These characteristics deal with how we should treat others. It is also a process of maturation as we journey in this Christian life.

It is important to view the gifts of the Spirit working in cooperation with the fruit of the Spirit. The gifts of the Spirit represent the power of God and the fruit of the Spirit represent the virtue of God. The virtue and power must work together to be effective, if we want to mature in God. We must align our lives with God's nurturing hand. The cultivation of the fruit is a byproduct of a disciplined life. We need His help to get there. His teaching is a method by which we can arrive.

Chapter Eight is a discourse on the value of living in community with other believers. Living in fellowship with other Christians can be rewarding. Living in fellowship is one of the great joys of life. In many instances, we are closer to our brothers and sisters in Christ than our biological families. God designed it this way because in eternity, we will spend all time together as the great family of God.

God is preparing us on earth, for that great celebration and community in the new heaven and new earth. In this chapter, we examine God's method for His people growing together, loving together, and His plan for the ultimate family environment centered around Him.

Chapter Nine, talks about the propensity for propulsion. In short, this means are we growing in God. We have often heard

God's Method

that if you are not moving forward, there's no such thing as standing still, but that you are going backward. So it is in the Spirit. We cannot remain in a state of idleness concerning things of the spirit. You are either progressing and growing, or you are declining and backsliding. God has designed us that way both in the natural and concerning our spiritual maturation.

No one wants to talk about backslidden conditions. Much of the church is in a backslidden condition, which many times, starts at the head. Sadly, many new converts do not experience the adulation of the new birth for this reason. Complacency and the desire for wealth, fame and fortune has doggedly attacked the lives of grounded believers so much so that we lack joy which translates to new believers being robbed of the joy of the new birth. They look at the church and see just people trying to make it through the daily grind in pursuit of worldly aspirations. We cease to demonstrate the joy, peace and love that should be represented in the body that new believers can latch onto for hope in their own lives. Of this failure, the church must repent. God wants to revive leaders with His method to teach the congregation about the things of God. Romans 10:14 reads, *"How then can they call on the one they have not believed in? And how can they believe in the one of whom they have not heard? And how can they hear without someone preaching to them?"*

We need the word of God spoken to us, so that we can grow. We need to sit under viable, alive Christian leadership that will enhance our spiritual progress. We need to sit among the congregation of believers, learning to love one another and singing spiritual hymns to one another, so we can grow. We need to return to a vibrant prayer life. We cannot grow by watching the televangelist or merely listening to Sunday services streamed on the internet. We must be amid the congregation, upholding one another so that we can mature in Christ. Clearly, Christian growth is a by-product of following His method and thus for arising as champions of the faith.

The concluding chapter does not represent the finality of the matter. You may find some loose ends. However, I am sure that as you consider the chapters herein, you will unveil other valuable facets of the method, that you can apply to your own life for successful Christian living.

There is much to consider for your own personal reflection. In fact, please meditate for a few moments, on the end paragraph of each chapter entitled, **Consider**. The questions there are designed for personal reflection and meditation.

Indeed, our quest for victorious Christian living does not end here. There is so much that God wants to share with us that will lead us to abundance and heartfelt joy in this life. This is just the start of the roadmap to strength, satisfaction and purpose to bring glory to God and to be a blessing to all those with whom you come in contact.

May you embrace God's method of biblical principles that will never lead you astray.

God's Method

Chapter 1

The Reality of Being Stuck in a Dry Place

Psalm 63:1-8 O God, You are my God; I shall seek You earnestly; My soul thirsts for You, my flesh yearns for You, in a dry and weary land where there is no water. Thus, I have seen You in the sanctuary, to see Your power and Your glory. Because Your lovingkindness is better than life, my lips will praise You. So, I will bless You as long as I live; I will lift up my hands in Your name. My soul is satisfied as with marrow and fatness, and my mouth offers praises with joyful lips. When I remember You on my bed, I meditate on You in the night watches for You have been my help and in the shadow of Your wings I sing for joy. My soul clings to You; Your right hand upholds me.

An age-old question in Christianity is, "How do I live a victorious overcoming abundant Christian Life?" Many sermons have been preached that made us shout and dance, believing we could instantaneously change our circumstance from that of defeatism to that of victory.

Many books have been written, outlining steps towards spiritual and personal success, that borderline New Age philosophy and the effectiveness of positive thinking. We have attended countless conferences of renown preachers, evangelists, prophets and the like. Attendance at such conferences, promulgated the possibility [and dare I say the promise] of a bestowment upon us of impartation, that made us think, God was going to do all the work and put us on this path towards abundance wealth and fulfillment.

God's Method

Our attendance at many of the big ministry conferences have given us hope that tomorrow will be a better day. The prayer for the miraculous has been prayed. The affirmation of faith has been pronounced and we leave with a renewed attitude. We feel the spirit of release and victory in our lives, only to awaken to the reality of a new day with its old and new challenges. The truth is that many times our faith has been ignited but there is still work to do on our part.

In the days to come, we return to our usual daily grind and are left with the same question, "How do we get unstuck?" "How do I get out of this dry place?" Stagnation has been our bedfellow for many years. It seems nearly impossible to move from this place to a land rich with milk and honey and the dawning of a new day. When will the rivers of water flow? When can we experience true growth and victory? How and when will my spiritual thirst be quenched?

The truth is, God has already given us a plan and a method towards abundance and victorious Christian living outlined in His Word. It's not super spiritual as some suppose. The answers we seek are not hidden. What we must realize is that God has given us the tools needed to live purposefully, abundantly and victoriously. There is no instant bullet—but there is a divine strategy.

No amount of seed offering we sow can negate what God has mandated. No maneuver or ploy can negate what it takes to move toward the plan and purpose of fulfilled Christian living. Keep in mind, that His fulfilled purpose for your life may look quite different from that of others who are living within their purpose. Your pathway and ETA (estimated time of arrival) to get there may be just as varied.

Continued intimacy with Christ, in love, relationship and lifestyle, will ensure, that we experience true satisfaction and completeness in this life. The only way to get close to God and to live in the center of His will is by our complete surrender to His will and obedience to His encompassing love for us.

To experience the fullness of His favor and His presence, we must live close to God and not confine our spiritual connectedness to Christ to a mere Sunday morning salvation. I'm not saying that our spiritual connectedness rests in how often we go to church. What I am saying is that it does not begin and end with the invocation and doxology, respectively. The conversation must go beyond the Sunday church regime. Our connectedness resides in our ability to yield daily to the very being of who Christ wants to be in us and to us.

It is, however, a mandate to be an active participant in the local church that believes in the fullness of living the spirit-filled life as exemplified in the early church. The responsibility is ours to take on the spirit-filled life for ourselves. We cannot live in the shadow of someone else's intimate relationship with Christ. It is futile to expect the relationship that our grandmothers, mothers, spiritual fathers, prayer warrior aunts and uncles had with God to be transferred to and conferred upon us. Relationship is not an inheritance. Our victory comes by our own personal sacred alliance and lifestyle of worship with the Lord as our personal Savior and King.

God's Method

Temple Worship as a Type

Although, we live no longer live under the old covenant which was fulfilled in Christ (Matt. 5:17ff). Temple worship is a foreshadow of and sets the ground work for a new and better covenant of the New Testament. What does that mean? It means, we can learn from how God set up temple worship and the priestly obligations of daily and annual worship on behalf of the people of Israel.

Old Testament worship was not a whimsical or haphazard affair put together on the precepts of emotionalism. It was a method of worship that the priests came into the holy of holies. There was a standard and an order that the priest came unto God. From this, we see how the priests were to come into worship of God. This can give us a glimpse as to how we are to worship God today. Although, we are not bound by the old Covenant strictness and rules, it does give us a shadow of how following His precepts opens the windows of blessings, flowing in our lives.

Leviticus chapters one through seven, outlines the five different offerings and directives to offer a proper sacrifice in the Old Testament. This is relevant to us today because it is a foreshadow and a type of New Testament worship.

First, it shows that worship was not a practice of convenience. It was deliberate in its preparation and execution. The worship was structured, and each function of the priest's role had meaning. Within Levitical worship, the priest was to bring an unblemished animal (lamb or goat) into the temple as a sacrifice to the Lord. The animal that he was to bring had to be void of any defects such as scarring. The point was to bring your best to the Lord as an offering to the Lord.

When we serve the Lord today, He desires that we too offer Him our best worship. This does not mean that we come perfect in His sight, but with a pure heart. This pure heart is paramount as to perfection before God, as we allow Him to sanctify us daily. In short, our worship should cost us something. It shows God's place in our lives; the place that takes priority over all else, including our own desire and our own will.

To give God first place over everything is to show Him our love towards Him and for Him. God desires a deliberate surrender and giving of our will to His will. That desire does not change. Everything that He does is to bring us into a loving relationship with the Creator.

Thusly, prominent principles regarding Levitical worship as it pertains to yesterday and today, is that God wants His glory (Lev. 9:6) above all else. We should worship the Lord Our God with all our heart, with all our strength, with all our mind. Secondly, He wants us to come to Him being thankful for all that He has done, for all that He is doing and for all that He is going to do. (Lev. 22:29) Give thanks with a thankful heart, give praise with a thankful heart. Thirdly, He requires us to be a holy people separated unto Him (Lev. 23:36). In the New Testament 1 Peter 1:16 reflects directly from Leviticus 11:44, *"Be ye holy for I am holy."*

Although we are free in worship today, because of Jesus' atonement for us, the Old Testament reinforces that God doesn't accept haphazard or sloppy worship from His people. We must serve Him with intentionality and obedience. Most of all with a passionate love, that comes above and before anything else. This

God's Method

passion only comes by knowing God for ourselves and developing a personal relationship with Him.

As we study the Bible, we can find that God has given us a method for spirit-filled victorious living. He has given us a method for completeness and wholeness that confounds mortal men.

The same expectation that God had for the church under the old covenant, is the same in the new covenant. It relates to our commitment and conversion to love God first and forsaking all other gods. These gods can and do refer to deities of any kind, including gods of the heart, (i.e., money, prestige, fame, sex, etc.). Anything that we worship, which takes the place of God, becomes our god. The Lord will not take second place to anything. He requires our obedience to Him in all that we say and do, period. This to some, may sound stern, but it is quite the contrary. His love for us is endless, but who wants a one-sided love?

The priests were also expected to be intercessors in prayer. We too, are expected to be prayer warriors for ourselves, our families, loved ones and those who test our love. The priests were also expected to live a spirit-filled life, not to be confused with those of idol worshippers or heathens.

You could tell the difference between those who belonged to God and those who did not. This expectation, is still in full effect for believers today. And finally, we are expected to have fellowship with one another. As the Israelites, celebrate the Shabbat, we are expected to fellowship (Koinonia) with one another today.

If we will work with God, He will work with us. We cannot get around His precepts. We cannot expect that one prayer service or the decree of one prophecy will automatically propel us into our destiny. We must first abide by what God has outlined for us as proper and acceptable worship.

When the next big conference comes along and you believe that you are finally going to get your breakthrough; think about if you are ready to follow God's precepts. Think about if you are following God's methodology, before you pay your money and go for the quick fix of deliverance, or to see a certain, prominent personality, who has already paid their dues or just may be the charlatan that has come to town with the nefarious purpose of derailing the road to your victory and leave town with his pockets lined.

Many god-fearing Christian leaders have paid their dues in prayer, obedience and sacrifice. We can't experience that same kind of victory and propulsion within our individual mandates and callings; if we aren't willing to submit to the same guidelines and operate in compliance to God's precepts.

Many of us have been in church for many years. As to my own experience, I have been a believer for over thirty years. I have been called out and received personal prophecy, more times than I can count. I used to write them down. I still do…sometimes. I try to keep them in a place where I can read them and check them off, if they have manifested.

My point is that from experience, many of these so-called prophecies, were very broad. They could have been pronounced over almost anyone. Few were on the mark and others I'm still waiting for the manifestation. I will say that I would refrain from allowing a single prophecy to influence lifechanging decisions,

God's Method

particularly prophecies, which I have no witness to, in my spirit. But that's another book. 😊

What is true for many of us is that there has been a gifting, a calling, a vision, a dream, a goal and a passion, that has been lying dormant for years. For some of us, for decades. We wonder, how do we get from the dream that is inside of us to the place of manifestation, letting which is inside, flow out. How do we birth it? Do we wait for a grandiose voice of God before we move? Do we step out because "we got the gift?"

Most of us have found out, that the answer is not on the outside of us, or in the form of leaders, pastors, mentors, etc. The mandate must come from within as a flowing river of water. It must be the spirit of God that is working on the inside of us, pushing us towards our destiny in Christ. Although our God-given leaders can many times be instrumental in the birthing process, the baby (dream, calling) begins in and grows inside of you.

It is the direct connection with God. It is through prayer and His spirit on the inside of us. It is His strengthening of us, giving us the courage, fortitude, humility and obedience, to move beyond what we can accomplish within our own strength to that which is super *(powerful, galvanizing, mountain moving)* natural. It is above that which we can do on our own. It is the birthing of the miraculous power of God manifested in the earth. In short, it is a divine push in our spirit that God orchestrates, only when creation is ready to receive what God has placed within us. It births within the perfect timing of God and not when we want it to.

Believe me, God knows how to get us in position for His glory to be revealed through us. It is the fulness of God's prescribed timing for us to come forth. We become ready to give, release and the recipient (world, persons, family), is in the place to receive. This was the case, when Jesus came into the world to be born, live and spread His message. Then, He gave His life and rose from the dead.

From His example, we see that we too, have a mission that sometimes does not depend on how ready we are to accomplish it, but on how ready the world is to receive it. We must wait on God's timing.

At the same time, God doesn't want us to live this life stuck in a vacuum. He doesn't want us stuck in mediocrity. He wants us to prosper in body, mind and spirit. Rejoice in the spirit of the Lord and be confident that this is the Lord's program. He will bring forth His purpose. He is never late. Rest and sleep easy knowing that God has you.

My prayer is that as you read the following chapters, you will find your personal key that unlocks a principle in your spirit, that sets you on the road to entering the life God has designed for you. Believe me, I have spent years learning some of the truths, that I share with you within these pages. I know that if you glean something that makes your road a little smoother and your load a little lighter, it was worth it.

Consider: Have you ever experienced a dry season in your life? Do you know the signs that you are in a dry place? Do you feel like you don't have any more to give? Or you just don't want to be in church, or much less serve on an auxiliary? Many of us

God's Method

in ministry had given for years and years. I personally have experienced this. You just want to take a break.

Have you ever just wanted to take a break? It's not that you don't love God. It's not that you don't love His people. You just need time to nurture yourself. Consider nurturing yourself, without guilt and pressure to continue doing. Some people call it burn out. It's okay to step back. Consider where you are in your spiritual walk. Consider where God has intended for you to be and examine if the two coincide.

It's okay to step back from the dry place, rest for a season, recalibrate and then move forward to a new place in Him. God can give us a time of refreshing. He may also want to change your course. Listen for God. There are times when we go through a dry place, that He is trying to change our season.

Chapter 2

The Catalyst of Conversion

Acts 3:19 Repent, then, and turn to God, so that your sins may be wiped out, that times of refreshing may come from the Lord.

As we attend church services throughout a given year, we hear a lot about justification by faith. But what does being justified mean? Eerdman's Dictionary of the Bible, gives us a succinct definition stating that "both the Hebrew and the Greek root of the word connote the meaning as being put "in the right [right standing] …with God."

Further, the writings of the Apostle Paul teach "…the principle… 'that no one is justified [made right] before God by the law.'"[1] Essentially it means that our (humankind's) good works cannot make us acceptable to God. Our benevolent actions and/or good deeds, cannot make us right before God and thereby give us entrance into heaven.

Only God's forgiveness, grace and atonement can do that. It's a common theme in Christendom. Only through Jesus' work of atonement (reconciliation) and our acceptance of Him as Savior, can we come into right standing with God. We can come before Him, blameless and spotless, because of His undying love for us through His work of atonement.

---

[1] Freedman, David Noel (Editor), Eerdmans Dictionary of the Bible, William B. Eerdman Publishing, Grand Rapids, MI (2000) p. 757-8.

God's Method

For many Christians, particularly new believers, this may sound like a lot of church dogma--a language that is reserved for the spiritual elite and/or those who attend bible college and seminary. However, this truth has significance for every person.

It's God's method of salvation for every person—for you, for me and for everyone who receives God's gift. In the church, we all had to come the same way, whether we have been saved for twenty years or saved for twenty minutes. Everyone must come to God in faith, accepting Jesus as Lord. This is God's gift of salvation, to draw humanity (those who will accept Him), back into fellowship with Him.

Throughout history, individuals have had to make a decision for Christ and further, we all had to surrender our lives to God. Upon making that confession, we all had to turn aside from our way of living and allow God to be the orchestrator of our lives. We all had to come to God with childlike faith, at some point in our lives, to gain a new and meaningful life in Him. We all had to come to Christ and ask Him into our hearts. We had to allow God to change us daily, sanctify us daily and transform us into His likeness. We all had to come by way of Christ's shed blood, His death and resurrection to be justified by faith and come to the realization of our spiritual identity in Christ.

The Apostle Paul wrote the book of Romans. Its main theme is justification by faith. Paul wanted his readers to know, that we all have fallen short of the glory of God. There is no man or woman, regardless of how many good works he or she has done, no matter how young or old, and regardless of your pedigree, how often you pray or give to the poor, how much philanthropic work you do, or how much you do with community service or activism. We all stand before God as sinners, needing to accept Jesus as Savior. Only by accepting Him and His shed blood (containing all redemptive power), can we be made right with God.

Not only must we believe *in* Him as being Divine, but also to believe *on* Him.   The difference is our surrender to His Lordship over our lives. We must give our lives over to Him in faith. The book of Romans addresses what makes one a believer and is a creed to Christian doctrine. Romans has been deemed as Paul's manifesto on faith—a primary and life changing method for spiritual reconciliation.

Romans 1:16-17, *"For I am not ashamed of the gospel because it is the power of God that brings salvation to everyone who believes… For in the gospel, the righteousness of God is revealed—a righteousness that is by faith from first to last, just as it is written: "The righteous will live by faith."*

Romans 3:28 reads, *"For we maintain that a man is justified by faith apart from works of the Law."* Paul expressed that it is only through the work of Christ, that we have access to the Divine. Our own works have no merit when it comes to the embarking of our spiritual journey with Christ. No matter how good the work, endeavor, or outreach is, it is not the strategy, whereby men can be saved. It is not the means by which, we can receive spiritual renewal and thus, have fellowship with God.

Romans. 4:5 *"But to the one who does not work, but believes in Him who justifies the ungodly, his faith is reckoned as righteousness,"*

Romans. 4:25, Who (talking about Jesus) *was delivered for our offenses, and was raised again for our justification.* Romans. 5:1 *"therefore having been justified by faith, we have peace with God through our Lord."*

God's Method

Romans 5:18 – *"Therefore as by the offense of one [judgment came] upon all men to condemnation; even so by the righteousness of one [the free gift came] upon all men unto justification of the Lord Jesus Christ;"*

Romans 8:30 *Moreover whom he did predestinate, them he also called: and whom he called, them he also justified: and whom he justified, them he also glorified.*

But I'm a good person, doesn't that count towards my salvation?

God loves us no matter our state. Because of His undying love for humanity, He created a method for us to have eternal connection with Him. Through our acceptance of that love in complete surrender to Him, we are granted access to the spiritual. Thus, we are granted eternal communion with Christ, in this life and forever.

We often hear that God loves the sinner but hates the sin. He has thus, through justification, given a method, whereby, humans may have relationship with Him. Plainly speaking, it is the way by which we are made righteous in the sight of God through faith alone, not by our own actions—not by works.

In the natural, it's like a person who commits a crime and who should rightly suffer punishment for his crime. But when you go before the judge, instead of going to jail, he drops all charges and gives you a clean record. Though we deserved conviction and to suffer the penalty for our crime, he erases it. It's as if it never happened and He (Jesus) throws our sins, in the sea of forgetfulness. Micah 7:19 states, *"He will again have compassion on us; he will tread our iniquities underfoot. You [Jesus] will cast all our sins into the depths of the sea."*

In Luke 15:11-31, we read the parable of the prodigal son, who sinned against his father. The son wasted what his father had worked for, scandalized the family name, and engaged in riotous living. When the son finally ran out of money and fair-weathered friends cast him aside, he realized the error of his ways and decided it was better to return home and be a servant of his father, rather than to continue in his waywardness.

Although the son caused his father great heartache, when he returned home, the father is overjoyed. He lovingly received him and didn't hold anything against him. As a matter of fact, the father throws a welcome home party for his son. A season of great joy filled the house. That is how God feels when we come to Him and take our rightful position as His sons and daughters.

Justification means, that God has dropped the charges for our sins. Those sins are forgotten by God and remembered no more. Ephesians 2:8-9, *"For by grace are ye saved through faith; and that not of yourselves: it is the gift of God."* I don't know about you, but I'm thankful to God for putting together a plan and method to draw me nearer to Him. He has forgotten every sin of my past to allow me to receive and experience His love and mercy. Despite my waywardness, indecisiveness and outright rebellion, He forgave me and allowed me entrance into His Divine love.

God's mercy allows us to receive salvation that comes by faith in Christ alone. We cannot earn it by doing good works. We cannot earn it by trying to live a squeaky-clean life. We cannot earn it on our own good deeds or on our own merits. We cannot buy salvation. Nor, can we work our way into salvation. All our best doing, our best living, our great deeds of compassion, all our social work and volunteering, doesn't get us into heaven.

God's Method

The time I helped my neighbor, doesn't make me right before God. When we took care of our friends' kids, as a favor to the parent while he or she was at school doesn't redeem us. The great offering, we gave to the church, doesn't make us right before God. The time that we were a good Samaritan and helped that lady on the side of the road, doesn't make us righteous. The confession we made to the priest in the confession booth or the reciting of the Hail Mary's doesn't make us righteous either. But you may say, "Don't we gain some brownie points with God for any of this?" The answer is "No."

The NIV translation of Isaiah 64:6 says, *"All of us have become like one who is unclean, and all our righteous acts are like filthy rags; we all shrivel up like a leaf, and like the wind, our sins sweep us away."* The New Living translation puts it this way: *"We are all infected and impure with sin. When we display our righteous deeds, they are nothing but filthy rags. Like autumn leaves, we wither and fall, and our sins sweep us away like the wind."*

Our philanthropic work, our fight for human rights (whatever we may deem that to be) and all our good deeds before the eyes of men, connotes that we are caring considerate people, with a conscious for the good of humanity. Don't get me wrong. These things are needed in society. God does use these devices to help humanity. But as for eternal salvation, the only thing that gives us right standing with God, is committing our lives to Him, believing in Christ, and accepting Him as Lord and Savior. The only thing that makes us right before God, is surrendering our lives to Christ and living a life of faith in Christ.

The Importance of a Surrendered Life

What does it mean to surrender our lives to Christ? Let's first look to the dictionary, to see the everyday meaning of surrender.

> "...**to yield** (something) to the possession or power of another...to give (oneself) up to some influence, course, emotion, etc... to give up, abandon, or **relinquish** (comfort, hope, etc.) ...to yield or **resign... in favor of another**..."[2]

From a biblical context, both surrender and sacrifice, means to relinquish or to yield to God's supremacy, power and control over our lives.

Romans 12:1 Therefore I urge you, brethren, by the mercies of God, to **present your bodies a living and holy sacrifice**, *acceptable to God, which is your spiritual service of worship.*

For many of us, we have felt the prompting of Christ, attempting to get our attention and engage us, on numerous occasions. He has been trying to draw us nearer to Him for many years. In response, for so long we continue to rebuff that tug on the heart and continue to brush off God's call for us to surrender to the Spirit's leading. We sing songs and claim that we want God's will manifested in our lives, but to do so requires a relinquishing of the desires of the carnal man. We can say, that to surrender to someone or in this case, God, is to relinquish/yield, our will over to God's will. For many of us, it means to stop

---

[2] www.dictionary.com, retrieved August 24, 2017

God's Method

fighting and ignoring God's authority over our lives. He is still trying to get our attention.

Once we have made a commitment to follow Christ, God begins to change our hearts. It is at this point where the Holy Spirit begins to work on our character and nature to transform us. While we are growing in Christ, there is often a struggle. The struggle is between allowing our will to dominate our decisions, or renounce our plans to God's will. We can only achieve victorious Christian living, when we put aside our fleshly desires and turn it over to God.

Justification is the method whereby, our relationship with God is initiated. Justification is the jumpstart of salvation. It is at the threshold of our salvation. It is us turning from our sinful nature and giving into the faith life that God summons us to.

Sanctification is the method whereby that relationship is kept alive. Sanctification is the day to day method of cultivating intimacy with God and through which growth in the holy things of God manifests. The work of sanctification is the alternator that keeps the spiritual relationship engine running and propels us forward on our journey.

God has justified (given us right standing with God) us with our initial conversion experience when we accepted Christ as Savior. He also sanctifies us (which means to make us holy) daily. Each new day, presents new opportunities for us to draw closer to God with life lessons that He orchestrates. What spiritual life lesson is He teaching you today?

Transgressions that once seemed okay to us now prick our hearts. Our desire is not to do them anymore. God sensitizes our hearts, at the onset of our Christian journey. Our hearts become very receptive and tender when we first receive Christ. We want to please Him. We become mindful of God's presence with us. We don't want to return to a sinful outlook on life and lessen the Spirit's ability to work in our lives. At our initial conversion, God gives us strength to obey His commands and turn away from sin.

Think about your spiritual surrender in the context of fulfilling your purpose in God. Our purpose and our yielding to God's will, are directly related to each other. It is connected to our success or our failure concerning the things of God. We may think our purpose is fulfilled in something that we like to do. But, our purpose may be fulfilled through our obedience to another vehicle of gifting that has been dormant or that we shy away from. Conversely, we may be on the right track for our ministry effectiveness with God's pruning hand and our complete surrender.

Consider: Reflect upon your initial conversion experience. What did you feel when you first accepted Jesus as Lord of your life? How long ago was that? Do you feel the same way you did when you first accepted Christ? Since that day, what change has there been to your outlook on life—your worldview? Are you reading your bible more and studying what it means to be in relationship with the Lord? When we embark upon our relationship with Christ, there should be a hunger to experience the divine in our lives. There should be a change in our appetite towards God, which only He is able to fill. As you continue to seek His love, He will fill it and show you His purpose and destiny for your life. As you surrender to Him, you will see a manifestation of God's intention for that which concerns you.

God's Method

Chapter 3

The Framework of Faith

Faith is the barometer of our walk in Christ. A barometer is an instrument, that measures the pressure used especially in forecasting weather and determining altitude. Let's break that down.

First, a barometer is a measure of atmospheric pressure. Likewise, faith measures how effective we will be in our spiritual strides in God. The degree of our victories are measured by our confidence in God and how we react (or don't react) to the pressures of life. Do we have faith in God during the difficult times? Do we have self-control when pressures come? Do we believe that God is for us?

Whether we are new to the faith or have been walking with the Lord for many years; whether we are young or mature adults, pressures do and will come. As such, we are confronted with making decisions as to how to handle daily pressures. The decisions we make concerning some of those pressures can have lifelong effects.

We stand at the precipice of pressure, confronted with a decision to make as to what our response to the pressure will be. We can either have a carnal response or we can have a spirit-filled faith response. Daily situations can present us with pressures is as if we are standing at the edge of a cliff. We can either allow faith to sustain us from falling into a place that will ultimately cause us harm, or we can allow faith to sustain us and lift us high above harm, to keep us from falling into a pit.

God's Method

Giving into pressure can cause us to fall into a ravine filled with jagged edges that can cause injury to spirit, soul and body. The injury can affect us, on many levels. It can be an injury of despondency rejection, failure, insecurity, lost time, etc. The ultimate result does not lie in the plan of God for our lives. Giving in to pressure is a vehicle that can lead us away from the fellowship of God. Any misstep off this precipice, can result in loss of years to repair the resulting damage.

If we walked in total dependence upon God, He would sustain us. Often at a precipice, we often cannot see what lies at the bottom of that pit. If we should fall, we are engaged, with only what we can see. We cannot see the details of a valley experience. If we rely on the strength of God, if we have faith that God will not let us fall, if we depend on Him, we can avoid many missteps in life.

There is great benefit, in recognizing that tests will come. Not every day in Christ will be a mountaintop experience. Through every difficulty, lies the opportunity to learn a spiritual lesson. God will use that lesson, to refine our character.

Pressure happens when things don't go our way. And the fact is, pressure will always come, no matter what stage of life we are in. Things will happen opposite to the way that we have strategized them to occur. This lets us know that God is ultimately in control.

This pressure causes us to look to God and recognize that He is in control of every situation. He changes our plans, continually. God trumps our ideas, stops the presses on our editorials and revises our game plans, in the middle of the quarter.

What God is interested in, is our faith in Him, as the great strategist, editor-in-chief and life coach.

What He is really after is our hearts. He wants us to be victorious in life. His plan is that we are spiritually whole sons and daughters. He wants us to be complete in Him. We can only attain wholeness when we have faith in the Commander in Chief's supremacy, in all matters concerning us. Just as the barometer forecasts the future, faith in Christ, forecasts our future success in life and spirit.

Secondly, a barometer gives future trends based on may factors such as humidity, altitude, wind, etc. Sometimes, the wind changes the forecast, which causes us to query whether it's going to be a sunny day or if it's going to rain.

The barometer also estimates when the weather will change. This ultimately means, that there is a time, when we don't know what the weather will be. We don't know exactly what to wear. We don't know if it's going to rain in the morning or in the afternoon.

In like manner, there will be times when we are unsure of the what, when and how of a situation. We must have faith that God is the supreme forecaster and He can reveal what we should do in any weather system. We must have faith that He will give us the forecast of what is coming when we are able to handle the weather and the situations that may occur in our lives.

There are times when God is silently orchestrating the occurrences and situations in our lives. We wish God would hurry up and say or do something—anything. There are times when our faith will be stretched. We must stand still and have faith. We must know that He will move. He is already engaged in our

God's Method

turmoil. You don't know when and you don't know how. However, you do know, that He will move on our behalf.

> Psalm 46:10-11a *"Cease striving [Be still] and know that I am God. I will be exalted among the nations. I will be exalted in the earth. The Lord of Hosts is with us..."*

We stunt our spiritual effectiveness for the kingdom, when we don't believe in God. We do ourselves a disservice and disappoint the heart of God, when we operate in a constant influx of pessimism, doubt and unbelief. We can't allow God's silence to throw us off. Even in the silence, He is speaking through our circumstance.

I have always questioned the prophet, who says, that God is always speaking to them. We must remember that God is not wordy. God speaks to us, when it's necessary. He is concise. There could be tons of silent times in our lives. Many times, He speaks concerning a certain subject or situation. He is waiting for us to move, to obey, what He has revealed to us before He gives us further marching orders.

The weatherman normally will forecast the weather for tomorrow or for the week ahead. Our job at that point, is to prepare for the weather for the day. We would wear a sweater or a jacket. Maybe, sunglasses or an umbrella, depending upon, what the weatherman has forecast.

In the spirit, if God has given us a glimpse into the future of our lives, then we should prepare for it. We are to prepare for what God has spoken over our lives. For instance, if God has given us a word, saying that we will preach or teach; that is the forecast for the future.

Our job during the present season, between the actual manifestation of His purpose and the occurrence, is for us to prepare ourselves for the work or the weather ahead. If we are called to preach or teach, we should prepare ourselves accordingly. If we are to evangelize, then what are we doing to prepare for that manifestation? All this requires faith, that we believe the forecast and we believe the barometer for the occurrence. How much faith do we have for the manifestation to come in due season?

Lastly, the barometer, forecasts the weather and determines the altitude of the weather system. In the Spirit, our faith determines the altitude of how high and how effective, we will be for the glory of God. The Bible says that, *without faith it's impossible to please God. (Heb. 11:6).* Fear is the opposite of faith. When we walk in faith, we can do great exploits for God. We can reach heights that we cannot reach in the natural.

Faith as a Life Changer

Primarily, our new life in Christ, begins with the act of faith in Christ Jesus and our acceptance of Him as Lord. God has called us into a personal relationship with Him. Ephesians 1:4 reads, "*...For He [Christ] chose us in him before the creation of the world."*

When we accepted that invitation, we opened the door of our hearts to Christ and allowed Him entrance. We not only believed that He was Lord and Savior, but we accepted Him as Lord and Savior. Anyone can believe He is Lord, in fact many people do. It is quite a different thing to accept Him as Lord of our lives.

As we proceed through life, our relationship should deepen. As we mature, we should take on more of His

God's Method

characteristics. If we are still struggling with the same carnal issues we had at our new birth, then our flesh, has more mastery over the spiritual growth, than it should.

The Greek word for Lord is *kurios* (κύριος), which has several different meanings, but in most instances, always has the connotation of Master. (Matt 10:24, 1 Peter 3:6). What is pertinent, is that the New Testament conveys a new life in Christ, where Christ is the head of our lives. He is the rabbi (teacher) of our life and we are reformed, conformed and forever changed, when we come under His tutelage.

He is also the Master of our life who heals us, spiritually, physically and mentally. Luke 17 tells of the ten lepers who were healed by Jesus. I believe that they received full and complete healing, of all that ailed them. The scripture concentrates on the physical healing. People could see the demonstration of truth, that Jesus indeed, had the power to heal. In His healing instances, I believe, that they received the inner healing, that was not readily apparent. Jesus had great mercy and made their healing full and complete, even beyond which is evident to mortal men.

Jesus changed their lives completely. Jesus changes our lives completely. Situations in our lives may remain, but God changes us on the inside. Once we open the door to Christ, allowing Him to become Lord, He will lead us into a new walk of faith in Christ. Our spiritual eyes open. We see life and our purpose in life in a new fresh way. We begin to look beyond our carnal selves and look to Christ as the sustenance of our lives. Paul said, *"we walk by faith and not by sight." (II Cor. 5:7)* We must walk by His leading, to please Him. New life in Christ changes us in ways, that cause us to see everything in the light of Christ's worldview.

When I first accepted Christ as Lord, He planted His seed inside me. I was no longer the same. My ultimate desire was and continues to be, that I want to please God. This was a work of His spirit. He did something inside me, that gave me a yearning for Him. He gave me the desire to learn more about Him.

My journey continues. I am always wanting to learn more, always wanting to get closer, always wanting to feel more of His intimacy and more of His hand in my life. I don't know how He does it. I don't know how He transforms us at our conversion. The things that were important to us, seem to take a backseat.

All I know is that I am no longer the same person I was before accepting Christ as Savior. This is not to say that I do all things right. But as it says in the Psalms about David, I have a heart after God and my desire is to pursue Him.

I am confident that in that pursuit, He never leaves us alone. He sees all that happens in our lives. He sees all that we do. He is omnipresent, in all that concerns not only me, but in everything in the universe. He is always there. We can be confident that He stands with us, in every circumstance and situation in life. We also know, He is the orchestrator of all things, whether we agree or disagree, whether we like it or not.

The question has often been asked, why does God allow bad things to happen to good people? I assure you, I am not God and I do not know the reason why some things happen. What I do know is that we live in a sin filled world, left to man's own devices, wherein many times, we suffer because of our own ingenuity and quest for the unknown.

God's Method

Man's inventions are an impetus of power, give us fame, fortune, comfort and industry. Albeit, at the same time, we are destroying our own world. In so doing, we destroy ourselves, giving rise to our waywardness and irresponsibility to care for the world, that God has placed in our hands. At the same time, much of man's ingenuity has led to scientific breakthrough, that has helped mankind down through the ages.

In the beginning, God placed all on the earth in the hands of humankind. Adam was capable of his responsibility to care for the earth and enjoyed the favor of God. When Adam ate of the tree of knowledge of good and evil, he lost his ability to care for the earth that was bestowed on him by God.

> Gen 2:15, 17 &19, *"Then the LORD God took the man and put him into the garden of Eden to cultivate it and keep it. 17but from the tree of the knowledge of good and evil you shall not eat, for in the day that you eat from it you will surely die. Out of the ground the LORD God formed every beast of the field and every bird of the sky and brought them to the man to see what he would call them; and whatever the man called a living creature, that was its name."*

During these changing times, only God can save man from himself. There is a steadfast immutability of God, that seeks us out, knocks at the door of our hearts and that draws us closer to Him. This is the engagement that will carry us throughout eternity.

John 3:16 reads, *"that whoever believes in Him shall not perish, but have eternal life."* Quite simply, to believe is to have faith. Jesus is someone that we cannot physically see. However, we know beyond a shadow of a doubt, that He died for our sins. All things are possible in God and nothing is possible without Him. This faith in God, leads us to follow Him. Jesus told His disciples to follow Him. They immediately left all they had and followed Him.

Spiritual growth is indicative of our character, becoming more Christ-like, as time progresses. How can two, walk together, unless they agree? (Amos 3:3). He is forming intimate relationships with each of us, so that we can share in this love walk with Him and experience Him working on us and through us. As we take on His nature, our spirit man thrives. First Corinthians 2:14 reads. *"...but the natural man does not receive the things of the spirit of God, for they are foolishness to him. nor can he know them because they are spiritually discerned."*

Through faith in Christ, our spiritual man becomes awakened. In doing so, we are allowing God to lead the way. He sets our feet on a path that is sure and that will not fail. More and more we relinquish control to God. It is not always apparent, how things will come together.

God wants us to learn how to trust Him. We don't understand everything that God is doing, or how He is doing it. God never promised that He would explain every nuance of our growth process to us. What we do know is that He is moving in us and changing our very nature. He is the God who we can trust with our lives.

Only a life in faith has the privilege of God's transformative power. His strength, enables us to put off the old man and put on the new. Although we have received Christ, there is another part of us that needs to progress towards trusting God and not leaning towards our own understanding. Yet, the seed of

God's Method

Christ has been planted. Jesus said, *"… if you have faith the size of a mustard seed, you will say to this mountain, 'Move from here to there,' and it will move; and nothing will be impossible to you."* (Matt.17:20) That mustard seed faith, will grow and will aid in our spiritual growth, as we walk with Christ.

This is precisely what God desires for us. He wants to be a father to us and for us to depend on Him, just as children depend on their earthly father. Childlike faith is what He is looking for in us. Although, He is not afraid of our questions and can handle any of our misgivings, He is looking for us to trust Him unconditionally, knowing that He wants the best for us. We can achieve a life that is guided by Christ wherein we yield to His guidance and prodding hand.

Faith, therefore, is the first step in our spiritual development, that continues to grow over a lifetime. Rick Warren mentions other steps for spiritual growth, that I think are worth noting: (1) Nurture growth with God's word (2) Cooperate with God as He prunes; and, (3) Pray through the 'Fruit of the Spirit.'[3]

There comes a time in life when our faith is tested. Life can sometimes deal us a blow that can cause our faith to be shaken. Pessimism and skepticism are the opposites of faith. A pessimist views the glass as half empty. An optimist views a glass as being half-full.

Negative attitudes work against faith and moves us out of position with God. For example, even Jesus our Lord desired to heal and to do many miracles in Nazareth, which was His

---

[3] Warren, Rick, Pastor Rick's Daily Hope, Three Steps Towards Spiritual Growth, http://pastorrick.com/devotional/english/3-steps-toward-spiritual-growth (May 21, 2015) [retrieved August 25, 2017

homeland. But because of their unbelief, He could not perform ~~the~~ many healings and set people free, even though it was His desire to do so (Matt. 15:58).

The release of miracles, healing, and power in the Spirit, is embedded in the degree of our faith. If you want to move mountains, you've got to have mountain moving faith. If you want to cross un-crossable rivers, you've got to have faith in God to cross over to the other side. This life will give us opportunity after opportunity to exercise our faith. Our faith increases, as we speak faith, as we confess faith, and as we practice faith. Thus, we become people of great faith. This is the kind of person, God can use greatly.

The bible is full of people who had great faith and did great things because they trusted that God would do just what he said and be faithful to His promise concerning them. God is looking for people of great faith in this generation. Would you consider yourself to be a person of great faith? Do you believe not only, that God CAN do anything, but that He WILL do anything for you? As His beloved children, His love towards us abounds. Even in a world of skepticism, there is one thing that is certain—great faith in God can still move mountains.

Consider: To what degree do you have faith in God and to what degree can God have faith in you. Can God trust you in the small things—to be faithful over that which He has entrusted to your care? And do you trust that God cares about every area of your life? If not, then what steps can we take to increase our faith walk? Remember, the more we spend time with God, the greater our faith walk will be.

God's Method

Chapter 4

The Obligation of Obedience

Although, only faith in Christ can save us, God still wants us to live peaceably and to obey His laws. Some believe, the new covenant abolishes the Old Testament laws, but Christ said, *"Do not think that I came to abolish the Law or the Prophets; I did not come to abolish, but to fulfill (Matt. 5:17)."* As such, the Ten Commandments can be a guide for living. Obeying them, is a byproduct of a transformed life. Further, each of the Ten Commandments is referred to in the New Testament. It remains relevant to us, as guidance, for ethical conduct for Christian living today.

Let us look at the context, in which the Ten Commandments in relationship to the transformed life of the believer, can aid in worship, that is acceptable to God.

1. **You shall have no other gods before Me.** There is only one God who came to us in human form. His name is Jesus. Peter, James and John, were scolded by God when they wanted to make three tabernacles, one for Jesus, one for Moses and one for the Prophet Elias. The Lord said, *"This is my beloved son, hear ye him"* (Matt. 17:1ff) Luke 4:8, *"You shall worship the Lord your God and only Him shall you serve."*

2. **You shall not make idols.** Proper worship is exemplified in our adoration, respect and adulation of God, through His son Jesus. To worship idols or graven images or

God's Method

saints, is anathema. The veneration of saints, idols or any supposed deity other than God (YHWH, El Shaddai, Jehovah, Emmanuel) I Corinthians 10:14 ... *"flee from idolatry."* is forbidden.

3. **You shall not take the name of the LORD your God in vain.** The words that we speak can either bless or condemn. Our words can breathe life to our lives, or bring a curse upon our heads. We must begin and end with speaking praise to God. The Lord wants us to speak well of Him. To speak well of God is to give Him praise and worship. This worship blesses Him and blesses those who speak it. When we speak ill of the Lord, we are cursing ourselves.

There is power in praising God. Many people believe that praise and worship service is used to fill in time prior to the preacher taking the platform. Praise and worship is really an opportunity for people to shower God with honor and praise, from our lips to God's heart.

4. **Remember the Sabbath day, to keep it Holy.** God is so desirous of a love relationship with humankind that He wrote in His commandments, that a day be set aside where we come together and collectively honor Him. Every day is to be holy unto the Lord, not just the seventh day. God expects us to be a holy people, a peculiar nation every day. He transforms us by His spirit daily.

He does rejoice, when we gather together, take time for family, friends, and church. He also rejoices, when we get away for rest and take a break from the daily grind of work. The Sabbath was created for man to rest. Mark 2:27 reads, *"The Sabbath was created for man, not man created for the sabbath."* Barnes Notes on the Bible, writes this commentary concerning the sabbath: *"The sabbath was made for man - For his rest from toil, his rest from the cares and anxieties of the world, to give him an opportunity to call off his attention from earthly concerns and to direct it to the affairs of eternity."*[4]

5. **Honor your father and your mother.** The Bible says, *that if we honor our fathers and our mothers, we will add years to our lives* (Eph. 6:2). Conversely, if we curse and ill-treat our parents, then we shorten our lives. Whether we viewed our parents' upbringing of us in a positive or negative light or whether it was non-existent, we should show them respect. Not because of their actions, but because God has laid down a commandment to be adhered to, concerning them.

We will always be a winner, free of guilt and at peace in our spirit, if we yield to His leading concerning them. So whatever resentment you have against your parents for whatever the reason, let it go or seek to resolve misunderstandings, so that your lives will be long and blessed.

6. **You shall not murder.** We may not murder with our hands, but many of us murder with our mouths, by gossiping and slandering the reputation of our brothers and sisters. We need to get a handle on our speech and our thought pattern, which is the genesis of our evil speaking. As we allow God to speak to us through His Word, we will see our speech evolve from a cursing to a blessing.

Matthew 5:21:22 *"You have heard that it was said to those of old, 'You shall not murder, and whoever murders will be in danger of the judgment,' But I say to you that whoever is angry with his brother without a cause shall be in danger of the judgment."*

---

[4] Barnes Notes on the Bible concerning Mark 2:27, http://biblehub.com/commentaries/mark/2-27.htm ,

God's Method

7. ***You shall not commit adultery.*** As we live a life towards Christ, He begins to change our appetite from unscrupulous, profane desires and seeks to purify our hearts and minds. As the process continues, He replaces our desires, with what He desires for us. God can help us to temper our fleshly appetites, if we let Him. There may be times, when the old man tries to re-emerge. Our overarching stance should be a love of God, the things of God and a desire for what He wants for us. Mark 10:11,19, *"So He [Jesus] said to them...'You know the commandments' Do not commit adultery."*

The story of David and Bathsheba in the II Samuel 11 and the following chapters, lets us know that because of David's misdirected affections, he suffered violence within his home and family for the rest of his life. Were a few moments of pleasure worth it? What God has for you, it is for you and we will not have to attempt to steal what rightly belongs to someone else. This is an age-old story, that still has relevance today.

8. ***You shall not steal.*** When we take possession of things that don't belong to us, it is an offense to the Lord. I know, there were times, that I had to put things back in the supply closet, at the office. Even something as insignificant as a pen, even though, no one was around. The Lord sees all. It's as if, He was standing there saying, *"Put that back! It doesn't belong to you"* Then, I began to reason. I'm not going to hell for a pen. (Lol) It's not worth it. I can go to the dollar store and buy a pen. I put that stuff back. Eph. 4:28. *Let him who stole steal no longer, but rather let him labor, working with his hands what is good, that he may have something to give him who has need."*

9. **You shall not bear false witness against your neighbor.** Integrity begins with, being a person who tells the truth. *"Life and death, are in the power of the tongue"* (Prov.18:21). When we lie, we permit the spirit of demise, to come within our sphere and curses upon our lives, our loved ones and those with whom we have connection. When we speak truth, we attract blessings and the favor of God, upon our own lives and the lives of others. Eph. 4:25, *"Therefore, putting away lying, "Let each one of you speak truth with his neighbor,' for we are members of one another."*

10. **You shall not covet.** Desiring what others have, is akin to jealousy. It is apparent, when we cannot rejoice in the success and blessings of others, but instead we desire to possess their good fortune. We want, what they have for ourselves. Luke 12:15, *"And He [Jesus] said to them, 'Take heed and beware of covetousness, for one's life does not consist in the abundance of the things he possesses."*

These ten commandments are part of the Old Testament Laws of Moses. Although, obeying these laws does not save us, they do represent a continuing code of ethics for our conduct and for Christian fellowship with one another. We will however, find that as we are being sanctified, in our daily walk with Christ, He teaches us daily lessons that are congruent with these standards of conduct.

As such, He helps us to live a holy life, yielded not only to His commandments, but draws us closer to Him. We need to hear His voice and live a life that is pleasing to Him.

Each day is a new opportunity to draw closer to God, with life lessons that God orchestrates for our growth. The sinful actions that once seemed okay to us, now prick our hearts and we

God's Method

don't want to do them anymore. Our hearts become tender and are acutely receptive to Christ.

We want to please Him. We need to be mindful of God's presence within us. We don't want to return to a sinful outlook on life and lessen the Spirit's ability to work in our lives. In our new conversion, God gives us strength to obey His commands.

Only faith in Christ can save us. However, God still wants us to live peaceably and to obey His laws. Some believe that the new covenant abolishes the Old Testament laws. Christ said that, *"He came not to abolish the law, but that he came to fulfill the law* (Matt. 5:17)."

In the onslaught of spiritual relativism where doing what feels right is the social normative, it would do us well, to give place to the commandments in our lives and to remember that there is a standard for what is right. These precepts do not change, through the thousands of years of their creation and are yet, relevant to us today. And, of course, we can't forget that Jesus said, that these commandments are summed up with *"loving others as we love ourselves."*

Isn't it interesting, that our relationship with others is a direct reflection of our relationship with God? We cannot please God, without loving our neighbors right. We cannot please God without doing right by all people, no matter what they have done to us and regardless of our feelings towards them. Nowhere in the Bible does it say to only treat people right, that treat you right. On the contrary, the Bible says, that forgiveness, is always in order.

Give Yourself a Break and Forgive

I know, it can be hard sometimes to forgive. Doing so, is part of our obedience to God. Grudges that we may hold, no matter how justified our feelings may be, ultimately holds us down in every area of life. What helps is, that forgiveness releases the other person of transgressions, committed against us.

God has given us that gift and continues to give us that gift, when we fall short of deserving that forgiveness. His grace towards us, should lead us to have grace towards others. Additionally, forgiveness is a gift to ourselves. When we release others of ill-treatment towards us, we release ourselves from bitterness and resentment. When we refuse to forgive, it unknowingly, affects many of our other relationships.

Our conversations become negative instead of positive. Our outlook is pessimistic rather than optimistic. We believe the worst in people, which can result in us living a secluded and guarded life. We turn, towards a life that is untrusting and isolated, all because we refuse to release others, when we perceived that they have wronged us. We also become susceptible to sicknesses of body, mind, and spirit. The toxins that unforgiveness releases in our bodies, can make us sick and cause us to die before our appointed time.

Again, once we accept Christ's invitation to new life, we are sanctified by the blood of Christ. We have allowed Him, to enter our hearts and to transform us. We are being made holy, as we walk with Christ, daily. He teaches us lessons, that draws us closer to Him. He helps us to live a holy life, that is yielded not only to His commandments, but draws us closer to Him, so that, we can hear His voice and live a life, that is pleasing to Him.

God's Method

Consider: The ten commandments have stood the test of time. They have guided the conduct of many generations, although there are many more commandments contained in the Torah. Do the ten commandments still have relevance in your life? Does God still want us to obey these commands even though the law is fulfilled in Jesus? What is interesting about these commandments is that although they are written down, there is an innate feeling that even if the ten commandments were not engrained in modern society, we somehow know that going against these precepts is improper conduct towards God and towards our fellow man. Regardless of how people try to discredit them, their ethical validity continues to be a path to righteous living. Thus, their credence cannot be denied.

Chapter 5

The Persistence of Prayer

Gen. 32:26-30 Then he said, "Let me go, for the dawn is breaking." But he said, "I will not let you go unless you bless me." So, he said to him, "What is your name?" And he said, "Jacob." He said, "Your name shall no longer be Jacob, but Israel; for you have striven with God and with men and have prevailed.... So, Jacob named the place Peniel, for he said, "I have seen God face to face, yet my life has been preserved."

We as believers, can become content with engaging with other believers, going to church and doing good works. We can become busy doing ministry work (i.e., singing in the choir, ushering, hospitality, etc.).

Before we give our service, He desires our heart and no amount of service, can take its place. In fact, for us to be fully effective in Christian service, we must have a strong prayer life. We must grab the horns of the altar and cry out unto the Lord, to make us holy and fill us, with His precious Holy Spirit.

In the old days, we used to lay at the altar and wait for God to meet us there. That seems to be a problem these days. We live in an instantaneous society. Everything has got to be right now. We don't believe in putting our time in with God. We don't wait on the Lord anymore. Many of us tend to run ahead of God's pace, which can lead to failure, frustration and confusion. If we pray for fifteen minutes and nothing happens, we are content to continue with life, and then get mad when things don't work out the way WE planned.

God's Method

I believe the Lord wants us to want Him more than anything, even to the point where it requires our time. He wants us to desire Him above all else, even about the purpose, plan and future, He has for us. He wants us to love Him more than anything—our gadgets, phones, social media, money, honey, possessions, aspirations, people, etc. You name it. He desires to be our first thought, not an afterthought. We must be intentional about our relationship with God. That is where so many of us are missing the mark.

Remember your first sweetheart? You and your "bae" would talk on the phone for hours. Sometimes, you didn't have anything to say. You would just listen to each other breathe on the phone. You did it, because you were in love with the person. You just wanted to be near them and spend time with them.

That's the kind of love God wants from us. He wants us to sit as His feet and bask in the aroma of who He is. God wants us to spend time with Him, at the altar. The altar means sacrifice. It is a place of sacrifice. It is a place of holy intimacy with the One we love.

We need to get a tenacity like Jacob, who was crying out to the Lord. He said, *"Lord, I won't let go until you bless me"* (Gen. 32:26). We need to get back to laying on the altar before God. We need to wait on Him, until He meets us there.

We need to wait on Him until we hear from Him and until He fills us and changes our very nature. We gain so much, when we sacrifice our time and spend it with God. When we spend time with Him, He works miracles in our mind and spirit that would otherwise take possibly years of consultation with professionals to resolve. Consider some of the ways God can transform us when we lay before Him.

1. *At the altar, the Holy Spirit rids us of anger*
2. *He heals our disappointments*
3. *He converts our minds and changes our nature*
4. *He heals us of church hurt*
5. *He heals us from the wounds of molestation*
6. *He heals our emotions from unholy relationships*
7. *He strengthens us for future battles and gives us insight about dangers ahead*

At the altar, which is the place of self-sacrifice, He does the work that no doctor, no psychiatrist, and no psychologist can do. We spend thousands of dollars trying to get fixed, when what we need is an altar experience. If we would just take the time to seek Him, He can help us where we thought we couldn't be helped. We just need to take the time to know Him in prayer.

Sometimes, we won't even know the words to say. He knows what we need before we say it. He understands and will meet us at the point of our need. If we can just draw close and call on the name of Jesus, He knows just want we need, before we call on Him and before we ask.

The Holy Spirit prepares us for the work ahead. Each one of us is designed for a special task, that we have been fashioned by God to undertake. However, some of us think, that we were merely saved, for our own enjoyment. Understand that, while our salvation is personal, it is also communal, in that we must share the good news with others. We were saved to make a difference in the lives of others and to bring people to Christ.

God's Method

We are His witnesses in the earth. He wants to fill us with the Holy Spirit and prepare us for the work ahead. We can't be ready to minister to the needs of others, unless we are empowered from on High. We can't be ready, unless we have sacrificed our own ambitions. We must allow God to replace our selfish goals with His Holy ambition, to help save others from the clenches and trenches of sin.

Prayer is conversation with God. It is us talking to God and God talking back to us. During this spiritual conversation, the Lord speaks to the heart of what concerns us. Because He created us, He knows just how to effectuate deliverance in the deep recesses of our souls.

Prayer is the lubricant that keeps your spiritual motor healthy. Prayer must be present from start to the finish. Mark 1:35. *"and in the morning, rising up a great while before day he went out and departed into a solitary place and there prayed."* When we begin our day with prayer, our steps are ordered throughout the day. Jeremiah 33:3 reads, *"Call to me and I will answer you and tell you great and them searchable things you do not know."* With an attitude of prayer, God speaks to us, the things that cannot be known naturally. He gives us direction and warnings. He consoles us and leads us in a way that honors Him, blesses us and others.

Many believe that God is aloof and not concerned with our daily struggles. But to the contrary, God is involved in every facet of our lives, if we allow Him. He cares about matters that concerns us, large and small. Through the practice of prayer, we open the door for God to get involved in our situations. We only need to invite Him in.

When we have ideas, or we are thinking about doing something major in our lives, many of us get excited. I know I have. The temptation is to go forward, without the direction of God. The trouble comes when we go forward without the sanction of God. We are saying, "God, I got this. I'll take it from here."

When our plans don't go as we thought they should, that is the time we come back to God and want Him to get involved. Sometimes, God's silence is a 'No' and sometimes God's silence is a 'Yes' but wait. In our society today, no one wants to wait for anything and that includes us Christians.

Many of us went ahead of God instead of bathing our plans in prayer beforehand. Then when we realize we have missed the mark, we come to God and midstream, we want Him to get involved. When will we learn to trust Him from the onset?

We need to trust God from the beginning. It would save us a lot of heartache and wasted time, if we began our aspirations, only after seeking God's sanction, guidance and approval. We must be willing to stop the presses, if God says no and forbids us to go forward, with our supposed, great idea.

I personally think of all the times I've gone ahead of God, only to make a mess and had to come back and start all over again. God knew my journey. Although, I wonder, how much I could have accomplished for the Kingdom and as a legacy, had I been more focused in my younger days on solely getting direction from God in prayer.

I try to tell young people my testimony, when I have the opportunity. My hope is that it will help them lead a life that is focused and bathed in prayer. I hope to encourage others to put

God's Method

God first, in all things. However, each person must live their own life. We cannot live it for them. No matter how much we desire our loved ones and mentees to learn from our mistakes. They must travel their own road. We can only pray that they come out on the other side blessing God.

The pursuit of God regardless of our feelings.

We must get to a place in God, that when everything around us seems to be failing and dreams seem slow to manifest, we remain faithful to God. Even when it looks like all is lost, God is here. We must have what the old saints would call "a know so salvation." What that means is, that no matter what comes or what goes, and no matter who comes and who goes, our trust and faith lies in Jesus. It means that we are committed to this Christian walk, all the days of our lives and nothing can turn us around. Do you have a "know so salvation?" Are you committed to seeing your Christian walk through to the end?

Let us testify to one another of God's great compassion and love for each of us. Trust that God is the great architect of our lives and although, we do meet resistance and challenges to our progress in Christ, we grow through every trial for, *"It is in Him, that we live and move and have our being."* (Acts 17:22) Our faith becomes strong, when believers testify of the victory of God, in their lives. Our faith grows when we hear how, God has provided for and healed them, time and time again.

We know through the testimony of others, that if God did it for them, He can do it for us. Testimonies strengthen our faith. We should hear testimonies and give testimonies. During our prayer time, we must confess the faithfulness of God, regardless of our feelings. We must affirm during our prayer, the sovereignty and the goodness of God, regardless of what we are going through. Our words have power. Proverbs 18:21 says, *"Death and life are in the power of the tongue, and those who love it will eat its fruits."* That's why affirmation is so important.

Affirmation is a declaration that we speak. It is a pronouncement many times before manifestation that God's promises in our lives, will come to pass. It is a verbal expectation, into the atmosphere, to let everything in the universe know, that the promises of God are Yea! And Amen (It is so). We speak the goodness of God and our situations shift, under the power of what we speak. God has given the authority unto the believer.

The enemy tries to fight our prayer lives, because of the power it represents. Prayer can wreak havoc on the devil's plans for humanity, in and out of the church. Unfortunately, the church as a house of prayer, has transformed into something other than God's intended spiritual sanctuary, in far too many instances, in modern days.

For this reason, many of our churches are weak and become more akin to social halls. We need to regain our passion for the Holy. God wants a vibrant church—one that He can recognize as the household of faith. We can only have life in the church when we commit ourselves to consistent fellowship with God in steadfast prayer, praise and worship.

For many congregations, the prayer service (if they have one), is the least attended activity of the church. This can be attributed to the actuality that the prayer lives of many in the church, is nearly nonexistent. The most fervent spikes in prayer are during times of calamity. Being pressed by the vicissitudes of life, many find themselves seeking supernatural intervention. They

God's Method

desire the miraculous to take place, wanting God to be a genie in a bottle who will come out of the bottle, only when summoned, to grant our three wishes. Receiving answers to prayers doesn't work that way.

The climate of our day, necessitates the consistency of prayer in our lives. We won't be able to live a victorious spiritual life without its practice as normative. We won't be able to win spiritual battles, that manifest in the natural, without engaging in a meaningful prayer life. The Bible says, *"If we pray behind closed doors, whether that be at the altar of the church or an altar in our homes, that He will reward us openly"* (Matt.6:6).

Prayer is at the center of our spiritual success. Without prayer and the Holy Spirit alive and well in the lives of each believer, there is no possibility of a church that is spiritually alive. This is one of the reasons the enemy fights prayer so much. He realizes that through prayer, we experience God.

The Holy Spirit meets us in prayer in a very intimate way. A way in which no amount of preaching and head knowledge can bring. We must experience Christ and His method of us experiencing Him as Spirit touching spirit. Head knowledge, bible study, seminary, and preaching, help us to understand biblical principles through the mouths of men, which is different from God touching man through His Spirit in prayer.

Further, it's time out for the prosperity gospel. It's time out for slick clichés. It's time out for feel good messages that leave us empty, unchanged, ineffective, and spiritually weak. It's time out for praise team after praise team, with no oil and merely displaying vocal aerobics and vying for church celebrity-ism. Time is overdue to get back on our knees, back to the altar, back on our faces and cry out to God and intercede on behalf of our families, church, nation and this world.

Prayer should be the main event at church. However, overwhelming numbers of churches have overlooked this important facet of the Christian walk. I believe that with all that is going on in the world, God is bringing his people back to a place of prayer.

Strong and fervent prayer warriors will fill the earth. Technology will aid in believers, coming together from all nations. It will be as it was on the Day of Pentecost, but on a larger scope. All the people of God, were gathered together, seeking the Lord for grace and direction. Just as Christ did at that time, He will move in us and through us, collectively to manifest His purpose on the earth. It won't be about individual agendas, but about God's plan, being manifested in the earth. This leads us to the Holy Spirit's place in our spiritual walk.

Consider: Think about the quality and quantity of your personal prayer life. Do you have a set time and place that you spend with God? While we can whisper a prayer to God at a moment, at any place and at any time, the value of disciplined prayer cannot be overstated. Think about taking a few moments each day to make entries in a prayer journal where you can trace God's answers to prayer. It makes us more reflective to do so. It makes us more aware that God is actively engaged in our lives and He is concerned with all things concerning us.

God's Method

Chapter 6

The Person of the Holy Spirit

To truly be led by God, we must be filled with the Spirit. For how can we know that which we are unfamiliar with? When we intimately connect with the Lord, He can lead us into all truth and the ultimate purpose for our lives.

To be filled with the Spirit, is to be charged with His power. Interestingly the Harris News Poll found as follows:

> "...a strong majority (74%) of U.S. adults do believe in God, this belief is in decline when compared to previous years as just over four in five (82%) expressed a belief in God in 2005, 2007 and 2009. Also, while majorities also believe in miracles (72%, down from 79% in 2005), heaven (68%, down from 75%), that Jesus is God or the Son of God (68%, down from 72%), the resurrection of Jesus Christ (65%, down from 70%), the survival of the soul after death (64%, down from 69%), the devil, hell (both at 58%, down from 62%) and the Virgin birth (57%, down from 60%).[5]

---

[5] The Harris Polls, Americans Belief In God, Miracles and Heaven Declines http://www.theharrispoll.com/health-and-life/Americans__Belief_in_God__Miracles_and_Heaven_Declines.html (December 16, 2013)

God's Method

Many people in the world want to believe that God exists and makes a difference in our lives. Just as Jesus did miracles for the people in the early Church, we must have that same kind of power with God, so that men will people have an opportunity to believe today. John 14:12, *"Truly, truly, I say to you, he who believes in Me, the works that I do, he will do also; and greater works than these he will do; because I go to the Father."*

Today, many Christians live on the outskirts of the manifestation of miracles and healings, that God wants to do in the earth. Why does this lack exist? Why don't we see the miracles of the early church today? This is a question that needs further study and to which we need answers. I do not claim to have all the answers. One thing I am confident in is, that God's spirit abides in those, who are intentional about their relationship with Jesus.

Christians cannot claim that they have an undying love for God, when they place so much emphasis on worldly things. G od works through those who have an abandonment for the evil pleasures of this world and allow Jesus to be Lord over their lives. *"No one can serve two masters; for either he will hate the one and love the other, or he will be devoted to one and despise the other. You cannot serve God and wealth."* (Matt. 6:20).

In short, we cannot be a fleshly carnal people and expect to see the manifestation of spiritualty, that testify of God's grace in our personal lives. Until a soulish abandonment occurs in our lives, we will not see the change in the United States, that could be the impetus for new life for our nation. Conversely, the Spirit dwelling in us is what attracts people to Christ. The Holy Spirit empowers us to be effective witnesses and spiritual servants in the Kingdom. God gave us the Holy Spirit because He knew man would need His power to be victorious in a world that grows further away from Him.

The Bible says that there would come a time, when people would call that which is evil, good and conversely this which is good, evil. In this time, we need God's sustaining power. He has given us the opportunity to be led by God, by infilling us with His very presence, in the person of the Holy Spirit.

From the beginning of the New Testament church, the Apostle Paul encouraged the church to be *"filled with the Spirit."* (Ephesians 5:18) This same directive remains true today. God yet wants His people to be filled with the Spirit. He wants what's best for us. Not to be filled with the Spirit is less than what God wants for us. God wants the best for His children.

Many people believe, that being filled with the Spirit began and ended with the Apostles of the early church (cessationists).[6] The problem with the cessationist point of view is they deny that the power of the Holy Spirit is active today to aid in personal and collective victory in the life of the believer. They reject that the same empowering person of the Holy Spirit that existed in the early church is involved and alive in the church today.

---

[6] www.theopedia.com/cessationism Cessationism, in Christian theology, is the view that the miraculous gifts of the Spirit, such as healing, tongues, and prophetic revelation, pertained to the apostolic era only, served a purpose that was unique to establishing the early church, and passed away before the canon of Scripture was closed (comp. 1 Cor. 13:8-12 with Heb. 2:3-4). It is contrasted with continuationism, which is the view that the miraculous gifts are normative, have not ceased, and are available for the believer today.

God's Method

It was during the time of the Apostles Paul, James, Peter, John and the other apostles, pastor-teachers, evangelists, prophets, sisters and brothers, that the same power that God gave to those in the upper room, is alive and manifests in the lives of believers to this present day.

The Holy Spirit is alive today and helps us to live a Godly life. He helps us to live a life pleasing to God. He convicts us of sin. John 14:26 reads. *"But the Comforter, which is the Holy Ghost, whom the Father will send in my name, he shall teach you all things, and bring all things to your remembrance, whatsoever I have said unto you."*

During Jesus' final days, He spoke to His disciples, candidly, about being put to death and rejoining the Father in Heaven. Although this was sad news to the disciples, He explained that it was necessary for Him to leave. He further explained, that He would not leave them comfortless. He would leave a helper, a comforter, that would stand alongside them (Paraclete) and help them to go on living a life of victory in Christ. The Holy Spirit is promised by Jesus and as such, the Holy Spirit will help the believer today.

The Holy Spirit testifies to humanity that Christ is the Sovereign Lord over all. As such, He has all power over good and evil; over the angels, good and bad; and has defeated satan by the death, burial and resurrection of Christ. The person of the Holy Spirit, who dwells in the believer, has authority and victory over sin through the Holy Spirit who resides within. Christ has provided a method through His atonement whereby we can have victory in this life. This is not gained through the law, but through faith in Christ with the culmination of a Spirit-filled life.

The personification of the Holy Spirit in the daily lives of believers has further benefits in manifesting the renewal of the mind and testimony of the grace and mercy of God through Jesus the Christ "the anointed one." In short, we are heirs of God's kingdom. The Holy Spirit in our lives is evidence that we have a great inheritance of that which pertains to God.

The Holy Spirit is not only our paraclete (walking alongside us), but also indwells us. He makes our spirit His home—Holy Spirit touching human spirit, living in us and through us. 1 Cor. 6:19 reads, *"Your body is the temple of the Holy Ghost which is in you."* The Holy Spirit resides within us, helping us to live; helping us to cope; helping us to rise above situations and circumstances and ultimately, to live in victory over the enemy.

The Holy Spirit emboldens us and helps us to be courageous when situations say we should be weak. God helps us to be filled with courage. He is our adrenaline in the face of danger and adverse circumstances. He gives us the boldness that allows our lives to testify of the revitalizing work of Jesus in the life of the believer. He gives us strength even when our natural man questions that reality.

Just as the martyrs of the early church, He gives us the grace to be bold in the faith even when it costs us everything, including our lives. This fact reminds me of the modern-day martyr, pastor and theologian, Dietrich Bonhoeffer, who was put to death at the end of World War II by the direct order of Adolph Hitler.

Bonhoeffer was hanged on April 9, 1945 because his testimony and activism for Christ stood in direct contradiction of the Nazi agenda. In fact, Bonhoeffer was part of a small sect (the

God's Method

Canaris group) who sought to put an end to Hitler's atrocities and nearly succeeded. Prior to his death, Bonhoeffer was brave and continued to teach Bible study while being imprisoned. At the end, an eye-witness to his death recorded that:

> "I saw Pastor Bonhoeffer ... kneeling on the floor praying fervently to God. I was most deeply moved by the way this lovable man prayed, so devout and so certain that God heard his prayer. At the place of execution, he again said a short prayer and then climbed the few steps to the gallows, brave and composed. His death ensued after a few seconds. In the almost fifty years that I worked as a doctor, I have hardly ever seen a man die so entirely submissive to the will of God."[7]

Indeed, Bonhoeffer was a courageous disciple, who could not have sustained a decorum of peace and ultimate surrender to the purpose of God in his life without the spirit of God dwelling within. He was filled with the Spirit which enabled Him to stand, even to the point of death.

Further, during slavery, reconstruction, and the civil rights movement, many Blacks suffered great sins against humanity and would not have been able to survive without the help of the Holy Spirit.

---

[7] Biography online, Dietrich Bonhoeffer Biography, http://www.biographyonline.net/spiritual/dietrich-bonhoeffer.html

Seasoned saints, during times of great tribulations and injustices would gather together in church services and house gatherings, where they would gain strength from the power of being united together (congregation of the saints) and would rejoice in singing the hymn *"Blessed assurance, Jesus is mine, O what a foretaste of glory divine...This is my story, this is my song, praising my savior all the day long."* That was the testimony of many church mothers that Jesus, indeed, lives and resides on the inside. Those dear saints had the seal of God upon their lives. No matter what winds life brought, they knew they could trust God. They knew their lives were in His hands.

If you were poor, uneducated and Black (particularly in the Jim Crow south), you faced wrongs of many kinds. All you could do at times, was rely on the assurance that Jesus would deliver and sustain, no matter what troubles life brought. All you could do was to rely on God's Spirit residing within to uphold you in the face of danger. All you could do was to stand with an attitude of faith, thanksgiving and praise, because you knew that God would deliver His people.

The same could be said for the early Christians who were eaten by wild beasts at the behest of Roman imperials. God gave them strength to face certain death. While this may not be the climate of today's Christians, we face different challenges that requires a "know-so" salvation.

It seems, that with every scientific discovery, it causes many to question their faith in Christ—from the 200,000-year-old homo-sapiens skeletal remains recently uncovered in Africa, to the discovery of billions of solar systems, much like the one we live in. It can cause us to question the biblical text. But God is

God's Method

not shaken by our questions. We must have an assurance that God is God of and overall. Scientific discoveries constantly question the existence of God.

From questions about gender assignment and House Bill 2, to questions over why bad things happen to good people. It is the Holy Spirit on the inside who allows us to experience God on a personal level, as the only One, who can give us an assurance above and beyond, what our finite minds can comprehend.

Being Baptized versus being Filled

As we have discussed earlier, being filled with the Spirit is an essential part in God's method for the victorious spiritual walk of the believer. Without the aid of the Holy Spirit, we would only experience a shadow of His presence. God left His Holy Spirit for us to experience His presence in a fuller way, throughout history and in modern times. We can rest in the knowledge that He is yet with us.

I want to look at several translations of John 16:13ff, that can illuminate our understanding, of the purpose of Jesus sending the Holy Spirit into the world.

New American Standard Bible. (NASB)

*"But when He, the Spirit of truth, comes, He will **guide** you into all the **truth**; for He will not speak on His own initiative, but whatever He hears, He will speak; and He will **disclose** to you what is to come. He will **glorify Me**, for He will take of Mine and will disclose it to you. All things that the Father has are Mine; therefore, I said that He takes of Mine and will disclose it to you."*

The Message (MSG)

"But when the Friend comes, the Spirit of the Truth, he will take you by the hand and guide you into all the truth there is. He won't draw attention

*to himself, but will **make sense** out of what is about to happen and, indeed, out of all that I have done and said. He will honor me; he will take from me and deliver it to you. Everything the Father has is also mine. That is why I've said, 'He takes from me and delivers to you.'"*

<u>The New Revised Standard Bible (NRSB)</u>

*"When the Spirit of truth comes, he will guide you into all the truth; for he will not speak on his own, but will **speak** whatever he hears, and he will declare to you the things that are to come. He will glorify me, because he will take what is mine and declare it to you. All that the Father has is mine. For this reason, I said that he will take what is mine and declare it to you."*

The above scriptures are indicative that the purpose of the Holy Spirit is that He will be our guide into all truth. As our guide, He is our spiritual compass. He ensures that we are going in the right direction, enabling us to reach our potential of all He has placed in us.

He gives us pertinent information that will make our spiritual journey more meaningful and opens our understanding of who Jesus is. He will lead us through this earthly life, through a world that grows colder every day and continues to be desensitized concerning the things of God. As the world strays further away from the truth of the Bible, our assurance and joy remains secure and alive in the earth as we lean on the Holy Spirit to guide us.

The Holy Spirit is our Helper in prayer and worship. Romans 8:26 reads, *"In the same way, the Spirit helps us in our weakness. We do not know what we ought to pray for, but the Spirit himself intercedes for us through wordless groans."* Because the Holy Spirit glorifies and honors God, we are endowed with this ability to do so properly with His aid.

God's Method

It is always the Spirit's aim to exalt the Father in the earth and in the universe. The Spirit causes our passion for Jesus to intensify so that we may be intimately acquainted with God in fellowship through prayer. The Father is desirous of intimacy and fellowship with His people and the Holy Spirit is our helper.

The Holy Spirit is also a revealer to us in that he discloses to His people what we need to know for the cause of Christ. This has an element of the prophetic. The Lord will reveal in the Spirit what we need to know as it relates to matters of His sovereign choosing on the earth. He alone chooses what to reveal and how it is revealed in the earth. God said that He will give us dreams and visions, that we will see the Spiritual and then be revealed in the natural.

> Acts 2:17 *"In the last days, God says, I will pour out my Spirit on all people. Your sons and daughters will prophesy, your young men will see visions, your old men will dream dreams."*

We see the activity of the Holy Spirit throughout scripture. The Bible is the ultimate revelation of God to humankind. The Bible is also a record of the activity of the Holy Spirit in the church so that our faith will increase. It is through the testimony of the Holy Spirit in scripture that we know that He is active today. There are great prophecies recorded in the Bible which discloses future events in preparation for when we will be with Christ.

Many theologians debate the validity of scripture. Because of a misunderstanding and skepticism of the character of God and His plan for humanity, many weak translations of the Bible exist today. Further, weak translations can be attributed to archaeological findings of gnostic literature, heretical writings, pseudepigraphs and apocrypha. The preponderance of these findings lead many to believe that the Bible is nothing more than a mythical book of ancient fables and superstitious beliefs. This is one of the great deceptions, leading many astray and away from God's redemptive plan for humankind.

Our pursuit of God necessitates that we look beyond the natural and see with an eye of faith to realize that sacred scripture is God's gift to man. The ultimate purpose of the Bible is for us to know God and experience His presence. His ultimate purpose is to promulgate faith with the result of uniting humanity with Him throughout eternity. *"If the Spirit of him who raised Jesus from the dead is living in you, he who raised Christ from the dead will also give life to your mortal bodies through his Spirit, who lives in you"* (Rom. 8:11).

Let us be clear that when we speak of being baptized in the Spirit and being filled with the Holy Spirit. Over the centuries, there has been rigorous debate over what it means to be baptized in the Holy Ghost and/or filled with the Holy Spirit. Such debates, can mystify young believers and cause many to miss the joy of the gift of the Holy Spirit. We must remember that the Holy Spirit is a person who walks with us through life and indwells the hungry heart with a passion and fire for the things of God. Knowing this, would help us to stay on the right track.

Many would like to draw clear lines between the meanings, when it may not be all together clear. It isn't necessary to draw these lines. Some define being baptized with the Spirit as occurring at the time of redemption, when we initially commit our lives to Christ.

Being baptized into the family of Christ was first mentioned by John the Baptist, when he proclaimed that Jesus

God's Method

would come and baptize you with the Holy Ghost and with fire (Matt. 3:11). He was testifying, that Jesus would come and do many powerful transforming works that John did not have the capability nor the authority to perform.

The infilling of the Holy Ghost, has been deemed by some as a second work of Grace. This is taken from Acts 2 where the early church were in the upper room, on the day of Pentecost. The hundred and twenty were gathered in one place and they received the Holy Spirit. They all spoke with tongues (living languages) of the day [(Greek) heterais, glossaias, dialekto] (Acts 2:4). This event signified the birth of the church. This is recorded only once in the Bible. It seemed to be a one-time-only occurrence where the language in which the apostles were speaking, was understood by people of other nations.

There are two other occurrences in Acts, where people were being filled with the Holy Spirit. During these occurrences, they spoke not in other tongues (languages that could be understood), but in mystical unintelligible stammering of the tongue.

This is what we see happening today in Pentecostal churches. This is the experience throughout history from the early church until this time. We hear of people being filled with the Spirit, speaking in an unknown tongue, as opposed to a language that is understood by people in a foreign country.

Albeit, I have read about a sprinkling of people speaking in other languages, but that is far and few between. Speaking in unknown tongues was mostly lost after the early Christians until the Azusa Street Revival in the early twentieth century. It was a fresh wind, that fell upon the church.

In 1904-5 the Welsh Revivals in England, occurring a year prior to Azusa, felt the refreshing of God, with the infilling of the Spirit. Very few occurrences are recorded that included speaking in tongues. Their experience was described as boldness in the Spirit, flowing tears and fresh fire, because they had been mysteriously touch by God. Many would say that they had a genuine life-changing experience with God. Their experience of refreshing did not include an overwhelming manifestation of speaking in tongues.

In defense of speaking in tongues, the Apostle Paul encourages it. Primarily speaking in tongues is praying in the Spirit. It has been called "prayer speech." A language that goes straight to the presence of God. Through our prayer language, we can give the appropriate speech to God that releases answered prayers. It helps us to pray with spirit driven motives and a correct approach.

When we pray in tongues, we pray to God in a language that only God understands. The effects are deep and wide. It builds us up and strengthens us in the Spirit. 1 Cor.14:2ff, *"For if you have the ability to speak in tongues, you will be talking only to God, since people won't be able to understand you. You will be speaking by the power of the Spirit, but it will all be a mystery ... A person who speaks in tongues is strengthened personally...."*

Paul said, "if you have the ability", which means, that some may speak in tongues and others may not. The experience of the infilling of the Holy Spirit, may be evident, by speaking in tongues (ecstatic indecipherable utterance) by some, but not necessarily by all.

God's Method

It would do us well, not to get stuck on this issue. Our focus and energy would be better spent on *"loving God with all your heart, with all your soul and with all your mind"* (Luke 10:27). God will give us and has given us what we need to lead a life that pleases Him. He has given us fresh wind and renewed life that can lead to a consistent Christian lifestyle, where we love Him and love His people. This is what He wants and expects from his children.

Those who still have questions about the Holy Spirit should remember that there is a constant thread that flows throughout those who are lead and filled with the Holy Spirit—love God and love people.

The Experience of His Wind Upon Us.

God's presence is with us. We experience His drawing power to come closer and abide with Him. He wants us to be in the world, but not of the world—to be holy for God is holy and He only resides in a holy (set apart) vessel. His Holy Spirit infilling us, convicts us of sin and replaces our sinful nature with His holy nature. We must be filled and refilled again and again, so that we can abide in His presence continually. The holy fire purges us of our sinful nature. It is by this fire that we are sanctified during our Christian journey.

We have previously touched on the fact that many of our churches today are a mere shadow of what God had intended for His church. There was a time when holiness and righteousness were synonymous with the church. People believed that to be close to God, you had to live a holy life, separated and apart, consecrated for His pleasure.

This mindset has seemingly left the church. Those who speak and preach of God's holiness and that people are to be holy are deemed out of touch with the times. But God is still calling for a holy people. Hebrews 12:14 reads, *"Pursue peace with all men, and the <u>sanctification</u> without which no one will see the Lord."*

While the Bible confirms this fact, holiness seems to be an unpopular message these days. Thus, we are left with the church as a religious social club in some respects. The power and anointing of God has left the building.

We have come to a time when we must return to holy and righteous living. We can no longer straddle the fence with the world and call that which is good, evil and that which is evil, good. God still requires holiness from His people.

We wonder why we don't see the healings that we used to see. We don't see the mountains move that we used to see. This is all a result of our fellowship and coziness with the ways of a carnal world. God will not compromise His holiness and adjust His standards for us. We must come up to His with a willing, repentant and contrite heart. There is no Holy Ghost without holiness.

A Change of Speech

Loving God involves that which pleases Him and exhibiting the spiritual fortitude to refrain from that which displeases Him. We tell God, how much we love Him on Sundays. This kind of speech pattern, should continue throughout the week. We say things that lets Him know, how much we love and appreciate Him. That is the kind of speech, that those around us should be hearing from us as well. As we mature in God, we should be keenly, cognizant of the words that come out of our mouths, that would cause displeasure and offense to His Holiness.

God's Method

The deeper our relationship with God, the more we will seek to eliminate speech that is distasteful to Him and would cause His presence to withdraw from our lives. Our words reveal what's going on in our heart. When the Spirit of God is influencing our life, our speech will reflect this. We won't be engaging in gossip, sarcasm or speaking evil about others.

> *"...Be filled with the Spirit, speaking to one another with psalms, hymns, and songs from the Spirit. Sing and make music from your heart to the Lord, always giving thanks to God the Father for everything, in the name of our Lord Jesus Christ. Submit to one another out of reverence for Christ." (Ephesians 5:18-21)*

Pure Worship

Whether we sing, dance, or play an instrument, it should be pure, honest and from the heart. Anyone can praise God. But, only those who have special relationship with God can worship Him. Through worship, our hearts are warmed by the presence of God. We can sense His pleasure.

It is during times of worship when we forget everything that is around us. We can give God first place and He will intervene in our human affairs. He will give us comfort, light, answers to our problems, healing and a deep sense of His care and love for us. There's just something about worship that renews our spirit and makes our burdens light. During an intimate time of worship, God enshrouds us with His presence to protect, love and care for us, beyond the immediate experience. He works not only on the recesses of our hearts but intervenes in the natural to give us expedient and relevant answers to the vicissitudes of life.

An Attitude of Thanksgiving

Giving God thanks for all things allows us to experience His goodness and sovereignty. This doesn't mean that we are praising God for tragedies, but we praise God, despite the unwarranted difficulties that may happen that we don't understand. It does mean, that if God is good, then no matter how painful this life is, we can honestly talk to Him about it. God understands when our confusion and is not thrown off by us when we come to Him with our anger and frustrations.

We can also thank Him for being loving and good. When we're filled with the Spirit and yielded to Him, we also give preference to others by treating them the way we would want to be treated and submitting to his supreme authority in all that concerns us. *In all things, give God thanks for this is God's will, concerning you.* (1 Thess. 5:18)

There will undoubtedly be times when life does not seem fair. There will be times that we are hit with a heavy blow. We may question if we are ever going to recover. Giving God thanks can help in our recovery process. It is like medicine to a sick body because during thanksgiving, God wraps us and covers our hearts during difficult times. His love for us is expressed even when we must press through pain and all the while acknowledging that He is good.

The Holy Spirit's Work in Sanctification

Sanctification is where holy living comes in. Jesus told His followers that He would not leave us comfortless but that he would send the Comforter (John 14:18). The Holy Spirit has come to be our helper and advocate to aid us in living a victorious Christian life.

God's Method

John 14:15-16 & 25 says *(15) "If ye love me, keep my commandments." (16) "And I will pray the Father, and he shall give you another Comforter, that he may abide with you forever; (17) Even the Spirit of truth; whom the world cannot receive, because it seeth him not, neither knoweth him: but ye know him; for he dwelleth with you, and shall be in you..." (25). "But the Comforter, which is the Holy Ghost, whom the Father will send in my name, he shall teach you all things, and bring all things to your remembrance, whatsoever I have said unto you."*

In this familiar passage of John, Jesus foretells of the Holy Spirit coming upon the church as a paramount event in the life of the believer. Why did God find it so necessary to inaugurate the establishment of the New Testament church, with the induction of the Holy Spirit?

First and foremost, Jesus knew that the church would need His comfort, presence, power and Godly authority to be established and to last until the time of His return. The church needed and continues to need His empowerment to spread the gospel to a world of hardened and cold hearts. Second, Christ wanted to let the church know that He had accomplished His work on earth and returned to the right hand of the Father. The church can be confident that He is still tangibly present with us.

The Lord knew that throughout the centuries, the world would grow in waywardness and distant from the precepts of God. It will take a believer, bathed in the presence and power of God, to make a difference in the world and keep the essence and truth of Christ alive.

As the world gets farther away from Christ being present on the earth and the reality of His death, burial, and resurrection, God knew we would need the Comforter to be with us. In the modern world, the Holy Spirit alive in the life of the believer is the only way people will see Christ in the earth. Through the Holy Spirit, they see Christ alive in us, which is a testimony that draws men to redemption.

On a personal level, the Holy Spirit is our helper. God knew we would experience the enemy as we seek to draw closer to Christ. Christ comes in the power of the Holy Spirit to give us strength, comfort and power over the enemy in our daily walk. Before we go too far, there are other reasons for the Holy Spirit in the life of the believer. You may ask, WHY? I'm so glad you asked. There are at least five other reasons to being filled with the Holy Spirit?

1. The Holy Spirit gives us strength when we are weak. Our carnal answers to life's problems, situations and circumstances will never be successful over spiritual attacks designed to destroy us. When we are weakened from spiritual attacks and would otherwise rely on our own ingenuity, the Holy Spirit steps in and helps us to allow the strength of Christ to uphold us and see us through. When the Holy Spirit strengthens us, God gets the glory and we can claim no glory for ourselves.

2. The Holy Spirit teaches us the truth of Christ. The Holy Spirit is the only one who can change our outlook on life from that of the flesh to that of the Spirit. He disciples us as we seek more of God. As we read God's Word, the Spirit gives us the wherewithal to understand things of the Spirit and changes our hearts in the process (John 14:26; Rom. 8:14; 1 Cor. 2:6–14).

3. The Holy Spirit convicts us of sin. John 16:8 teaches that the Holy Spirit convicts us of sin to conform us to the likeness of Christ. The word convict comes from Greek word *elencho*

God's Method

(ἐλέγχω) which means "to convince someone of the truth; to reprove; to accuse, refute, or cross-examine a witness." The Holy Spirit convinces us of the truth that our sin is in direct opposition to God's holiness. He seeks to convince us of the ability of Christ to transform us from sinner to saint wherein we take responsibility of our sinful state and stand secure in the saving grace of God to change us.

4. The Holy Spirit reveals and empowers us for Jesus' purpose for our lives. The purpose of our life is to glorify Jesus through the power of the Holy Spirit and to love people. The Holy Spirit will reveal the finer details of our purpose, such as where we will work, in what capacity will we serve, whom we will marry, and where we will live, as we study the Bible and walk in faith.

5. The Holy Spirit works through prayer. The Holy Spirit will intercede for us through prayer (Rom. 8:26). He will intercede, when we're focused on glorifying Christ and loving His people. If you don't know what to pray, ask the Holy Spirit for help. After all, He is "the Helper" who will aid those who love Him. Oftentimes, God uses our prayers to change our own heart more than the hearts of others. He will also use our prayers to transform our way of thinking to be more like Him.

The Lord wants to give us this power and we need His power just as much as the disciples of the early church needed Him. The disciples were instructed after Christ's ascension, to wait (tarry) for the Comforter to come and endue them with power. This endowment was not just for the early church, but that same power is for us today.

Today, with evil on the rise, we need the indwelling of the Holy Spirit. With His power for living, God gives us direction and discernment about the issues of life. He gives us power over evil influences and the authority to subdue them. You see, the enemy doesn't want us to talk about the Holy Spirit. He does not want us to realize the power that has been given to us as believers.

We need to realize and walk in our God-given authority to make things line up in our lives. We have authority over every negative and evil influence over our lives, our families, our finances, our minds, our bodies and our spirit. But all too often, we refrain from that confrontation because of disbelief. Many are fooled to believe that the Holy Spirit really doesn't reside within us and give us power and authority in our everyday lives. We mistakenly believe that only the pastor and clergy walk in that kind of authority and that's just where the enemy wants you—feeling powerless and alone. It's a lie. Don't believe it. You too can walk in power.

When we are endowed with the power of the Holy Spirit, we have the power to move mountains. We have the power to command the winds and the waves and make them behave, all in the Name that is above every name and that name is Jesus.

In the Holy Spirit lies the power to change our very nature. The Holy Spirit gives us the ability to live holy. In the Holy Spirit, we have the power to live victoriously, free from fear, to cease from cursing, backbiting, lying, stealing, disrespecting our elders, and overcome every vice that the enemy would use to make our lives meaningless and to separate us from God.

The absence of the Holy Spirit's presence in today's churches, deems the social club instead of a spiritual house. The absence of His presence in our churches is the spirit of religiosity that causes churches to stand at the crescent of mediocrity, where

God's Method

everything and anything goes and at some point is DOA (dead on arrival). Some people say that holiness is irrelevant and that everyone can do what they FEEL is right in their own eyes. This feeling, (dare I say, heresy) will continue to lead the church astray.

The truth of the matter is that WE NEED the indwelling presence and power of the Holy Spirit. In a day like today, we cannot afford to live without the full package of His power resting on us and abiding in us. We cannot expect to be victorious without accepting the full embodiment of the Holy Spirit. God cries out for a holy people acceptable unto God, to be different and to make a difference in this world.

Consider Peter's exclamation in Acts 10:34, that *"God is no respecter of persons"* in the context of church practice today. It seems that there are in the pulpit who have greater access to God than those in the pews. In reality, we can all have the same access and experience the same presence and indwelling of the Holy Spirit because God is no respecter of persons. There is no big "I" and little "you". He loves all of us. He desires to have intimacy with each of us. Thank God we all can be filled with His presence. That depends on us and the depth of our desire to have intimacy with God

Power for Service

Acts 1:8 reads *"But you will receive power when the Holy Spirit comes upon you. And you will be my witnesses, telling people about me everywhere—in Jerusalem, throughout Judea, in Samaria, and to the ends of the earth."* This empowerment is both for personal relation as well as for outreach. It is evangelical in nature. The Holy Spirit empowers us to be a bold and courageous witness for God with signs and miracles following. It is the dunamis (gk. Δύναμις) power, might and strength of God, shown forth through us. The Holy Spirit, gives us the ability to be effective in doing God's will and to succeed in the work of God. It is also God's enablement for Christian service.

It is not only for effective service in the church, but to do the miraculous in the marketplace and on the streets where everyday people live. Very seldom do we read in the Bible that Jesus and the apostles performed miracles in the temple. They performed miracles where the people were—in towns and cities, on the streets and in people's homes.

It certainly takes courage and an unyielding assurance that God will meet us when we go out among strangers. It is the kind of faith that Oral Roberts and Katheryn Kuhlman had. They were giants of the faith. The challenge for the church today is to come out from the four walls of the church and to do more church without walls. We must be more open to utilizing new technology as tools to advance the gospel. No more church as usual.

Consider: Think about the thing that you know God has called you to. Are you walking in the purpose for which God has created you? There may be times when you don't think you have what it takes to accomplish the task God has given you. But, consider that God has given you His spirit, so that you will have the power and authority to aid in the deliverance of others.

The enemy doesn't want you to know that you have this power, but indeed you do. Stand in that knowledge that your contribution to the cause of Christ is what God has implanted in you to do. You are unique and you have duty to complete your assignment in the way that only you can. Walk in your authority.

God's Method

Chapter 7

The Fruit of the Spirit in Practice

According to 1 Corinthians 12:12ff, the Lord has given His Church spiritual gifts as a testimony to unbelievers and for the edification of believers. Many are familiar with the gifts listed in 1 Cor. 12:8-10,

> *"For to one is given the word of wisdom through the Spirit, and to another the word of knowledge according to the same Spirit; to another faith by the same Spirit, and to another, gifts of healing by the one Spirit, and to another the effecting of miracles, and to another prophecy, and to another the distinguishing of spirits, to another various kinds of tongues, and to another the interpretation of tongues."*

The gifts of the Spirit are for power to operate fluently and effectively in ministry on the earth. However, we need to be mindful that the Fruit of the Spirit mentioned in Galatians 5:22, love, joy, peace, longsuffering, gentleness, goodness, faith, meekness, and temperance should operate in conjunction with the gifts of the Spirit. Having the power gifts without the undergirding of virtue of the Fruit of the Spirit is a recipe for failure and will sooner or later bring about personal and public calamity. Without the two (power and fruit) working in concert in a Christian leader's life, there will be a personal reckoning and a waning of church reputation.

God's Method

The nine gifts are for power and the nine fruits, are for character. It is mentioned in I Corinthians 13, *"that above all, we must love God and love His people."* It would do us no good to have great power and not to exhibit great love. God gave His only son, because He loves us.

I have seen many ministers who have great and powerful exhibitions of healing and deliverance. However, on a personal level, their love-walk or the way they treat others does not match their power in the Spirit. God wants us to love and treat others right above all else. As we follow Christ and seek to be more like Him, we must check our fruit. We must do an inventory of the fruit we possess. Obtaining Godly character, cannot be complete without possessing, pruning and growing.

Humility and the realization that we have no power without God will help keep us balanced and to always be compassionate toward others. When we become self-absorbed, then we are walking in pride. This is when we cause others to stumble. This will lead to the pride that cometh before a fall. (Prov.16:18)

We must remember that gifts come without repentance. We may even be able to operate in these gifts with a measure of power. However, if we operate without the Fruit of the Spirit, we are counted unworthy and we miss the mark. Conversely, if we operate in the Fruit of the Spirit and have little manifestation of the power gifts in our lives, we can still win others to Christ and be a blessing to the community of faith.

In short, God wants us to possess the power gifts and the Fruit of the Spirit. They go together in our lives. It's a testimony of His goodness when we allow one to temper the other. God wants us to walk in the fullness of the Spirit. He wants us to manifest His power and He wants us to manifest His love.

Notice that in I Corinthians, the twelfth chapter, Paul delineates the gifts of the Spirit and immediately, in the next chapter, He talks about the love:

> 1 Cor. 13 1-3, *"If I speak with the tongues of men and of angels, but do not have love, I have become a noisy gong or a clanging cymbal. ² If I have the gift of prophecy, and know all mysteries and all knowledge; and if I have all faith, so as to remove mountains, but do not have love, I am nothing. ³ And if I give all my possessions to feed the poor, and if I surrender my body to be burned, but do not have love, it profits me nothing."*

Amazingly, right after Paul's dissertation on power, He says *"And now I will show you the MOST EXCELLENT WAY."* He is saying that love is better than possessing gifts. He is saying, it is more important, that we love. He goes on to say that though we exhibit the power gifts for all to see, it means nothing if we don't exhibit love. It's useless. It's just a lot of noise—a clanging cymbal*(1Cor.13:1ff)*.

We are nothing without the virtue of love exhibited in our character. We know that love is the summation of all the Fruit and all the law. Jesus talked about love in the gospels. He said that love of God and love of people is the fulfillment of all the law. Paul picks up on that premise, teaching the church about two principles working together--power and love. 1 Cor 13:4-8, *"Love is patient, love is kind and is not jealous; love does not brag and is not arrogant, does not act unbecomingly; it does not seek its own, is not provoked,*

God's Method

does not take into account a wrong suffered, does not rejoice in unrighteousness, but rejoices with the truth; bears all things, believes all things, hopes all things, endures all things. Love never fails; but if there are gifts of prophecy, they will be done away; if there are tongues, they will cease; if there is knowledge, it will be done away."

Paul preaches this same message to the church at Galatia. We see that love is a theme to all the churches throughout his letter. His premise is that by virtue of Christ's love for us and our love for others is the impetus for fulfilling God's will on earth. All people will know that we are Christ's because of love.

Galatians 5:22 mentions the first fruit as being love. The remaining eight Fruit of the Spirit are grounded in love. Love is joyful. Love is peace. Love is long-suffering. Love is gentle. Love is good. Love is faithful. Love is meekness. Love is self-controlled.

We've talked a lot about the Holy Spirit. The Holy Spirit is an integral part of God's method for grounding believers in the faith. God has provided love to bring us into the completeness of His provision for a fulfilled Christian life. I like the way Charles Stanley put it in his book, *"Living in the Power of the Holy Spirit"* where he states, *"The spirit-filled, spirit-led person is going to radiate exuberance for the things of God* (pg. 84)." I haven't met a spirit-filled person who was not excited about the purpose and promise upon their lives. They may not have it all together, but they have a heart for God and want to help others experience that kind of spiritual love relationship.

On a practical note, when we talk about growing in the gifts of the Spirit, we can reckon it to having an attitude adjustment in the spirit. Attitudes can have either a positive or a negative connotation.

Webster's defines attitude as, *"a settled way of thinking or feeling about someone or something, typically one that is reflected in a person's behavior."* From this, we can see that attitude involves how we think and how we feel, that results in our behavior. It is reflected in our outlook on life.

Lots of elements can contribution to our attitude. The bible teaches that our attitude must be conformed to embody the Fruit of the Spirit, no matter the circumstance. Our outlook should affect the circumstance; not the circumstance determining our attitude.

If we are a person of peace, love, joy, and longsuffering, and that becomes an innate quality in us, then regardless of what the situation is, those traits will manifest, because that is who we are. Only God can change our nature. Only God can change who we are. It can be an arduous process for some, but we sure can help Him out, by cooperating with His method. If we allow the Word of God to fill our minds and hearts, practice the discipline of the Holy Spirit, and spend time with God, we will evolve through His process of sanctification.

The Holy Spirit will help us pinpoint the direction we should take in life. He will aid in our attitude adjustments, if we let Him. The Holy Spirit will help us to know our purpose. He will guide us into all truth and the knowledge of the purpose and call within us. Without Him active in our lives, we are at a great

God's Method

disadvantage, because we do not have the ammunition to make a great impact for Christ that will set the enemy to flight.

Consider: Think about your responses to unwelcome occurrences this week. Can you remember your attitude and response? There will always be difficult situations and challenging confrontations that arise, but it would do us well to remember that God's plan for us is not made for our comfort. His plan for us is that we will be transformed in our hearts and minds to reflect His glory.

Chapter 8

The Fortitude of Fellowship

Even though we have a personal salvation through faith in Christ, it is not meant for us to walk throughout life in a state of me-*ism*. We are called a community of faith, which has the implication of a fellowship, sisterhood and brotherhood.

A healthy Christian walk is one that is inclusive of others. We are the family of God. There are no big "I's" and little "you's." All of us are an integral component of the family of God. We get into trouble when we lose the significance of that balance.

Many, particularly in this day of individual spiritualism, maintain necessary connections to the body of Christ. Many believe they can be a Christian by merely watching church on the television or on the internet. They believe by watching their favorite preachers on social media, be it Facebook, Periscope, Instagram, YouTube or whatever new media application that hits cyberspace, at the time you read this book.

We cannot adequately serve God without actively engaging with the family of God although many of its members have numerous idiosyncrasies and shortcomings. We are still family! The Holy Spirit unites us as a body of believers—the family of God. Families sometimes disagree. Family members sometimes debate, argue, dispute and question each other. The result should not be separation because we differ. Each member is unique, and we should be different from one another. However, we should remain united on that which we agree and

God's Method

that is, that Jesus Christ is the way, the truth and the life. No man comes to the Father, except by Him (John 14:6).

When talking about fellowship of the believers, a good expression of what that means, is the Greek word *koinonia* (κοινωνία). In short, it is the embodiment of Christian fellowship. This was the essence of the gathering of the early church wherein the communal meal was the center of worship. There are three aspects of koinonia which gives a fuller picture of what it means to be part of the family of God.

1. **Fellowship -** We are family. It is part of God's plan that we be one living, breathing organism, of the body of Christ. One Body, one fellowship, one baptism. True family cares for one another, serves one another, forgives one another, loves one another, prays for one another, laughs and cries with one another.

The church needs to remember, particularly during difficult times, that we are eternal family members—here on this earth and later in heaven, FOREVER. If we truly knew and believed that, we would treat each other with more tenderness and give thought before we utter an insult or slander. More effort and time, should be spent on building each other up and no time spent on tearing each other down.

I find that there are way too many cliques in the church which leaves people feeling left out, isolated and alone. No one should feel more alone after a church gathering than when they came in. However, this remains an unfortunate fact for far too many church-goers.

We have got to be purposeful in our fellowship by going beyond our immediate circle of friends and reaching out with an attitude of inclusivity. Too many fall by the wayside when we forget to love every family member. We need to create more opportunities for fellowship. Someone needs to know they are significant, that they matter and that they are loved.

Fellowship in the body of Christ is family. Acts 2:42ff says, *"They devoted themselves to the apostles' teaching and to fellowship, to the* **breaking of bread** *and* **to prayer.** *Everyone was filled with awe at the many* **wonders and signs** *performed by the apostles. All the believers were together and had* **everything in common.** *They sold property and possessions to* **give** *to anyone who had need. Every day they continued to* **meet together** *temple courts. They broke bread in their homes and ate together with glad and sincere hearts, praising* **God** *and enjoying the* **favor** *of all the people. And the* **Lord added to their number** *daily those who were being saved."*

From this verse alone, we see the many components of Christian fellowship:

They ate together. They prayed together. They experienced healings and miracles together. They shared with each other. They collaborated in missionary/outreach endeavors together. They praised and worshiped together. They visited each other.

They had a good reputation in the community. They worked together to successfully evangelize the community. *"For by one Spirit are we all baptized into one body"* (1 Cor.12:13).

Jesus said, that they will know you by your love one for another. Today, we are to practice that same kind of love for one another. We grew closer by shared experiences and spending time with one another. When we do this, it is a testimony to others that our love is genuine, and it inspires others to join a loving family of believers. Our example of fellowship, that attracts others

God's Method

to join us in the Christian walk, comes from the practice of the first century Christians.

2. **Participation:** They became part of the vibrant life of the church. As part of a church family, our participation in church plays out within society. The Christian culture and belief system is an example to the world of what it means to be redeemed by Christ and to be changed by the love of God.

As part of the church family, we should also allow the testimony of morality and virtue to spread out into the streets and into the communities in which we live. The Bible says, that we should be the salt of the earth and the light of the world.

We cannot assimilate into society and allow depraved social standards to become the norm within the church. Our faith will be tested, but we are stronger together. We have a voice, a moral compass and a spiritual aptitude for the things of God. We can reveal to our families, our cities and our nation, Godly precepts to bring about physical, mental, social and spiritual healings. Our participation, can turn our families around and set us on a tried and true foundation. But, if we are silent and refuse to let our light shine, we grieve God and those who would have heard our confession, remain unenlightened.

3 **Contribution and sharing:** The early Christians gave of their substance towards the mission of Christ. It was not given to build cathedrals or churches. Contributions were used to help the needy.

They gave willingly, as an act of self-sacrifice and not out of pressure or obligation nor did they give to receive the adulation of men or reciprocity of some kind. The ability to give and having the means to give is an honor and a privilege. We praise God that

He has entrusted us with enough to take care of our needs, our family's needs, as well as enough to help others. This is a great opportunity to share what it means to love others, not just by words, but as an act of worship.

Many churches in the United States are experiencing huge declines in membership. People are leaving in droves. Often, the issue is not with doctrine or the worship service. The issues are related to the fact that they don't experience the church in its purest sense of a family of believers (koinonia)[8] They don't feel a part of the body. They come in alone. Possibly, someone greets them at the door and they fill out visitor's cards. But essentially, they came in feeling unloved and leave the same way they came in. Or maybe they felt the love as a first-time visitor but after the first few visits, the lovefest and was not maintained and we lose them.

Many go as far as joining, but they don't feel connected. I believe that we (the church), need to do a better job making people feel like family, right from the beginning. Many times, church members spend a lot of time checking people out and vetting them, before they allow themselves to be known. We miss many souls in this observation stage. We deal with people pessimistically, instead of optimistically. If they don't look like us, wear the same type of clothes we wear, and more and more, if they are not part of the demographic (age, culture, etc.) that church leadership is trying to reach, they are left by the wayside.

---

[8] Strong's Concordance 2842, "communion, fellowship, joint participation; the share which one has in anything, participation…"

God's Method

Allow me to apologize to all the people who have been left standing on the edges of real church fellowship. This is not what Christ intended. There is a hymn that reads *"There is room at the cross for you. Though millions have come, there's still room for one, there is room at the cross for you."* Pastors, let's make everyone who steps through the church doors know that there is room in our church family for them. Regardless of how they differ; God makes room. Let us make room with outstretched arms.

Pastors and church leaders need to be the prime example of the shepherd who loves and cares for ALL the sheep. He or she needs to make sure that extensions of the ministry, make all who seek Christ through their ministry, know that they are loved and accepted and that they are an integral part of the body.

The Dangers of Isolation

I want to talk about how important it is that we live in community. We are our brother's keeper. We are our sisters' keeper. When we are weak, we can lean on one another, as family. We should be able to rely upon family members as breathing organisms. When we act as though we can operate independent of each other, that is when we run into trouble. Although we may be grown and have learned a lot in life, we will always need others to be healthy and whole.

The enemy doesn't want us to be healthy and whole, so he always seeks to divide us. How many times, are we at odds with our Christian brothers and sisters? Stand guard and know that the enemy seeks to divide and conquer. He sows seeds of discord that causes us to be at odds and saps away our strength, which causes us to cease to be strong and united in the faith. In his attempt to divide, he will also try to isolate the weaker ones, so that he can bombard them with a full assault. If we are not careful, we can become separated and ripe for a fall.

What is interesting is that the separation does not come in one swoop. We would recognize that and put our guard up. No, it happens slowly, progressively and without us recognizing it. We must be on the lookout for anything that would cause us to compromise our faith. The enemy will whisper that people don't love us when nothing could be further from the truth.

If we believe the lie, the stage is set and we move away from our sources of strength and those who give us wise counsel. Remember, the ultimate plot of isolation is to destroy you as well as your testimony. If he can't destroy us physically, he wants to destroy our reputation, our future, our ministries, and our destiny. It is all rooted in a demise of the believer. He separates us from our power base and seeks to keep us from impacting the lives of others with the gospel.

So, no matter how strong we think we are in the Lord, isolation can weaken us in long stretches of time. The menacing effects of isolation can begin with something so small as a whisper in our ear, "they don't like me." When we hear that, we have got to know, that it's a lie and even if that were true, we must rise above it saying, "He/she may not like me, but I love them." Say it aloud. Confess it and let your actions confirm it.

If we want friends, we must show ourselves friendly (Prov. 18:24). We can't sit in a corner, waiting for people to come to us. We need to go out and let others know that we desire fellowship. If you are anything like me, as an introvert I must sometimes tell myself that God didn't create me as an island. I've got to get up and go to lunch with the ladies, even if I don't know

God's Method

anyone. Go to the barbeque and meet some people. Make conversation with people and listen to others.

We are to live in community, singing spiritual songs and worshiping the Lord. It is not enough to watch the televangelist or to participate in online church. God did not create us to live apart with an illusion of family on the internet. We draw our strength and our joy from being with others. Presence is important. Just showing up to the party is half the battle.

All of us, have been burned by a relationship at some point in our lives. However, we must not let that hinder us from believing deep in our hearts, that there are good people out there, who will cherish our friendship as we cherish theirs. God is present in friendships. He was in the friendship of David and Jonathan; Paul and Luke; Elijah and Elisha; Job and Eliphaz, and; Bildad and Zophar. *Eccl. 4:10, "For if they fall, the one will lift up his fellow; but woe to him that is alone when he falleth, and hath not another to lift him up."*

Friends are a gift from God. Walking through life with others is a life with the love of family and friends. This is a blessing that will keep us grounded, balanced and happy. It is part of God's plan for wholeness in body, mind and spirit.

Consider: In this age of social media, the significance of true friendship can be lost. We share the best of ourselves online; we share emojis, pictures and quips. We accept friend requests on Facebook from people we barely know. However, real friendships require our presence and the sharing of our real self. Jesus' relationship with his inner circle (Peter, James and John) allowed him to share an intimate part of himself that he did not share with others. He allowed himself to be vulnerable, knowing full well that their humanity could hurt him, and it ultimately did. As believers, we sometimes put expectations on one another that does not allow for their humanity to come forth. As Jesus was disappointed by his friends, we can expect that it can happen to us too. We must never allow our disappointment in previous relationships to keep us from engaging in meaningful friendships with others today. God has created us to be in fellowship with other believers for we are stronger together than we are apart.

God's Method

Chapter 9

The Propensity Towards Propulsion

If you have walked with Christ for any length of time, there will be seasons when it seems as if our lives are at a standstill. I know for me personally, this is when it seems as if nothing is working. We have got to recognize such seasons as being a blessing in disguise. It is a time when God keeps us hidden, either for our protection, or simply to wait on His perfect timing to accomplish His purpose within us, for the good of others.

When this season occurred in my own life, it was very frustrating, because no matter what type of good ideas I had or what I tried to do to propel forward in a righteous cause (in my eyes), it was to no avail. I had to learn to rest in the timing of God. I could not force God's hand or ardently work towards a philanthropic goal because God had put on the brakes.

He did this not because He was punishing me for some wayward act. He did this because it was not in His timing for me to go forward. He kept me hidden. Jesus was kept hidden until His appointed time to go into ministry. During this time, John the Baptist baptized Jesus. It was not until God the Father had decreed and sanctioned that Jesus should begin His earthly work that Jesus' ministry began. So it is with us.

There will be times when we feel we are stagnate. But rest assured that God's timing is perfect, and we will move in the center of His will at the appointed time. During the time of God's hiding, God wants to show us Himself. He wants us to get to

God's Method

know Him and His ways so that when we are given our marching orders, we will then know how to conduct ourselves in a way that honors God.

Grieving the Holy Spirit

There are times, when there is the temptation and propensity to become complacent in our walk. When this occurs, we do not honor God in our daily walk. We act as if God can't see us when we do wrong. Also, our conversation can grieve the heart of God. We act as if God cannot hear us.

There is the tendency at times, to take the grace of God for granted. We cannot hide from God. He knows all. We sin, we ask forgiveness, we willfully sin, we ask forgiveness—and on and on, over and over. It's a cycle that grieves the Holy Spirit and causes more detriment to our Christian walk than we realize. It's not that God gives up on us. It's that we should know better by now. We should have matured and should be feeding on the meat of the Word. We should walk as adult children and not adolescent children, always needing correction and being told the same things over and over.

Yes, God will always love us, but we have got to grow up. God cannot use us if we continue to be childish; continue with secret sins and succumbing to the small fox holes in life. God knows all about that little white lie, the office supplies we took home, the indiscretions that we think, He doesn't know about, or the cyber sins committed on the private server of laptops, etc.

Small willful sins, grieve the Holy Spirit and we become our own worst enemy. It's not the devil. It's not that sister, who doesn't like us putting up roadblocks to our destiny. It's not that people of influence won't help us. It's a heart thing.

God will not advance us. To advance is to have the ear of God. To advance is to be trusted to move forward in fellowship, favor and with the power of the Holy Spirit. We cannot claim access to it because that kind of blessing requires that we walk in the power and the Holiness of God. We cannot possess that, when we continually grieve Him.

Eph. 4:30-31 *"And do not bring sorrow to God's Holy Spirit by the way you live. Remember, he has identified you as his own, guaranteeing that you will be saved on the day of redemption. Get rid of all bitterness, rage, anger, harsh words, and slander, as well as all types of evil behavior."* What does it mean to grieve the Holy Spirit? The Holy Spirit is a person. He has feelings as we do. What we do, whether we are in public or whether we are alone, affects our fellowship with the Holy Spirit.

The Holy Spirit corrects, chastises and sometimes disciplines us, when we are wrong. By the same token, when we are right, He rejoices with us. When we return to sins from which we were delivered, this too grieves the Holy Spirit.

In so doing, we don't have the intimacy with God that we would normally have. It's like, when someone we love has hurt us in some way or said something that offends us. The way that we regain re-entry into that special bond is to acknowledge our transgression. We need to fight the tendency to shift blame on others. We need to acknowledge it, own it, and repent of it.

You see, when we commit offenses against the Holy Spirit, negative attributes can multiply. Our attitudes are misaligned when we offend the Holy Spirit. We don't see things clearly. The enemy eschews our vision and warps our mind with the negative. When we grieve God, we go against His plan for us.

God's Method

We see things in a different light—a light that causes us to miss His blessings and opportunities to move forward in purpose and full life.

Offense the Enemy of Fellowship

We have spoken earlier of isolation and what it does in the life of the believer. Akin to isolation is *offense*. Offense is the primary foxhole, that satan uses to divide God's people and to stop us from walking in unity and reaching our full potential in Christ.

The enemy uses offense not only to keep Christians from Christ, but also to sabotage our relationship with God and make our lives of little or no effect. The enemy knows he can't keep us from being a Christian. So the next best thing is to keep us defeated, divided and disillusioned through offense. Offense is one of the biggest stumbling blocks in the Body of Christ. What keeps it going is that we fail to recognize its demoralizing impact.

We were made to live and work in the community. Even at the genesis of creation, God said, that it was not good for man to be alone. God created Eve so that the two, would be as one. The trouble came in the garden when there was strife between Adam and Eve after they ate of the tree of good and evil. Adam stated that it was the fault of Eve. Right in the beginning, there was disharmony—there was the strife.

That same tactic to divide and concur through strife, is the same ploy the enemy uses today. It's not a new strategy. It's as old as time. He continues to use it and we continue to succumb to it, making the army of God frail and of no effect. It causes all of us to stumble in our walk with God, as a body of believers and in our individual devotion.

The Sin of Taking offense

Ephesians 6: 11 – 13, *"Put on the full armor of God, so that you will be able to stand firm against the schemes of the devil. For our struggle is not against flesh and blood, but against the rulers, against the powers, against the world forces of this darkness, against the spiritual forces of wickedness in the heavenly places. Therefore, take up the full armor of God, so that you will be able to resist in the evil day, and having done everything, to stand firm...."*

I have been in church for a long time and in all the years that I have served, I have been offended more times than I'd like to remember and more times than I'd like to count. I often remembered and wallowed in the offense waiting for an apology that never came. Many times, I cried myself to sleep as the offender went on their merry way, not even realizing the hurt and deep wound that they had caused.

My fault and my responsibility in the offense was that I remembered it. I needed to cast it in the sea of forgetfulness, realizing that God forgave me repeatedly for sins I've committed. In that same manner, I needed to forgive people of the things they said about me; the lies they told about me; the jealousy that they had because of opportunities and blessings in my life. I held those things to their charge and I needed to forgive. So I continued hurting myself and others because hurt people hurt other people.

For many of us, it's hard to forgive when people have hurt us to the core of our soul. I know that many of us have heard the message, that unforgiveness hurts us more than anybody or anything. We sin against God and we sin against ourselves when we carry offense and refuse to forgive. It stagnates our growth and has no place in God's method of redemption and victorious

God's Method

living. It is counterproductive to what God wants to do and where He wants to take us.

I had a friend who continued to rehearse and talk about offense in her life. I agreed that she was correct. The sin that was committed against her was so imbedded in her mind and in her spirit that she was hurting herself by not releasing them of the offense. The effects of the offense was causing her to accomplish her own spiritual demise. She was now working against herself and her progress by allowing the offense to take root by rehearsing it in over and over in her mind and by gossiping and telling others about it, trying to get others on her side. I told her as, I often told myself, that she has got to find a way to forgive, so that she can be free to live and move towards her destiny.

The sin of *giving* offense *"When you sin against your brothers in this way and wound their weak conscience, you sin against Christ. Therefore, if what I eat causes my brother to fall into sin, I will never eat meat again, so that I will not cause him to fall"* (1 Cor. 8:12-13).

Many of us don't want to admit it, but there are times, when we have hurt people deeply. We have offended people, we have gossiped about people, and as Christians, we have wounded people to the core of their soul. We never attempted to apologize or to reconcile. Some of the people we have offended have gone on to glory with the offense still within them.

I charge you today with the help of God, that if there's anyone that you have offended and still have opportunity to reconcile, then do so with humility and love. If the offense is old, there are times both parties will have moved on and forgiveness has already been given. God has dealt with the situation. There is no need to revive old wounds. But you can go in grace and in love with an open mind and an open heart, as both parties walk in forgiveness. But more times than not, an apology is warranted. God will not release us to move beyond where we are until we have corrected our offense. No amount of praying, singing or shouting, will release us of our responsibility to get it right with our brothers and sisters. Go out for coffee...Have conversation...Give each other a break...forgive.

I know that I have been offended and I have offended many in my lifetime. For that, I'm deeply sorry. Today, I try to move on as an older person, reflecting on my life and vowing to walk in the spirit of love, not allowing an offense to take root. I vow to do unto others, as I would have them, do unto me.

Our offenses over time, whether given or received, have caused many setbacks in life. Offenses cause disharmony within the body. We need each other to go forward. We can't go on to do great exploits for God on our own, no matter how gifted, how talented, or how anointed we are. We need others to succeed in ministry and to fulfill our destiny in Christ.

Jesus needed the twelve disciples. Paul needed Barnabas, Titus, Timothy and his many fellow laborers, throughout his missionary journeys. Likewise, we also need to work with others so that they can fulfill their destiny in Christ. This is just as important as fulfilling our own destiny.

We can't be so selfish to see only our own destiny as needing to be fulfilled. We need to say, "How can I help my brother reach their full potential? How can I participate in their victory?" The one who is full of pride and competition, only seeks their own glory and seldom helps others to reach their destiny. We must walk, believing and knowing, that as we help others, God

God's Method

will help us. As we forgive others, God will forgive us. As we love others, we will gain camaraderie within the body that will help to propel us all forward.

Three Steps Toward Restored Fellowship
1. **Acknowledge sin**
   a. Admit the grievance occurred.
2. **Own the sin**
   a. I committed the offense. I did it.
   b. I allowed it to penetrate my heart. I embodied it.
3. **Repent of sin**
   a. I'm sorry, I was wrong. I will change my behavior.

Lastly, we must learn how to weather the storm. Because we are humans in relationship with one another, undoubtedly, there will be misunderstandings. We cannot live with our heads in the sand and think that we can live free of offense.

Offenses will happen, but we can be victorious in every incident. We must choose our reaction, be brave enough to humble ourselves and not let offenses fester. It may be difficult and a hard conversation, but it is something that can be done. After it is done, we can have a lightness of spirit, knowing that we have done our best to be loving, kind and forgiving.

Consider: We have undoubtedly been the cause and the recipient of offense on occasion. Think about the incident and whether it was reconciled. Is a conversation needed? Maybe yes or maybe not. An important question is, "Have we accepted our responsibility in the occurrence, whether victim or aggressor?" and, "What resolve have we made for the future to restore the relationship, remain in fellowship with our Lord and to free ourselves of offense?" In every stage of life, offenses will come. What matters is how we handle it when it does come and try to restore fellowship with all tenderness, humility and love. Life is too precious to hold on to offense.

God's Method

Chapter 10

A Matter of the Heart

The Church has been blessed over recent decades. Many Pastors make a comfortable living as a spiritual leader and even have paid staff that includes medical benefits. Indeed, we have seemingly been blessed if we look at the prosperity aspect of doing church. On the other hand, we have never been in such a place of spiritual lack as today. Saints are perplexed and confused concerning their personal lives. Countless clergy have exited the Ministry and chosen different careers. Online church is on the rise and we are inundated with the prosperity gospel rather than sermons preached for the spiritual edification of man..

Truly, churches are in trouble not because of financial reasons but because of a deficit in matters concerning the heart. Our hearts are in desperate need of revival. Our hearts are in need of refocusing and a reexamination of what it really means to be Christian—a follower of Christ, a disciple of the Lord and a lover of God.

In this book, we have dealt with some of the issues that draws us closer to God and these are biblical principles that, if followed, will undergird us with God's method of what the desires of our spiritual journey should look like. We can herein find fullness of life because it is the life that God has decreed for us to live. We will find our purpose and live in the center of God's will when we abide by His methods. We have all erred at something at some point in our lives. It's okay--God knew that we would, but the

God's Method

Lord wants us to get back on track. He can handle our shortcomings, but His holiness requires that we be renewed, revived and restored through repentance.

We need to find our place in God and work in that with all diligence and with a satisfied heart. This place may cause us to receive few accolades of men. But we will be satisfied if we do it for Him with a good attitude and for the right reason. Before we can walk in our calling, we need a complete surrender in our hearts. We need a redirection and to allow God to direct our paths and to set us on a sure foundation. If God doesn't build the house, those who labor, labor in vain and our endeavors will fail (Ps. 127:1). We will find ourselves exhausted trying to do what we think is right.

Many of us are in danger of losing our vision and purpose. We have been caught up in making money rather than winning souls for the kingdom of God. We are losing a whole generation of young people to the streets and to their own devices because our focus is amiss. They're not interested in our Sunday school lessons and they're not interested in what we have to say as they find much of what we say irrelevant to what they are facing in everyday life. But we can be the vehicle of change and the voice in the wilderness that so many need if we will follow what God has placed in our hearts and hands to do. Many of us strive to make our own little kingdoms out of businesses and parachurch organizations that have nothing to do with the evangelization of humankind. But God is calling for us to return the simplicity of His word and what He has called us to do. Much of what He has called us to is not surrounded in glamour and in church celebrity.

But God is calling for us to return to matters of the heart and to the saving power of the Gospel.

I have not offered within these pages any quick-fix solutions to arriving at our station of calling, but only encourage us to return to that which is tried and true--biblical principles that will strengthen our spiritual journey and compel us to reach others with Gospel of Jesus Christ.

God has not changed His purpose, neither has He reordered the mandate of the Church. We have changed in our attitude and actions toward God. We feel that God owes us something when it is us that owes Him everything. For Christ paid the debt, that He did not owe, and we owe a debt that we could not pay. By following God's method, we can recapture our zeal for God and His people. We can return to our first love—Jesus Christ and He will redirect our minds and hearts to fulfilling His calling for our lives. Through prayer and following His Word, God's vision and purpose will remain permanently in our Spirits, actions and attitudes.

Consider: Deut.6:5 says. *"You shall love the Lord Your God with All your heart, with all your soul and with all your might."* Think about all the aspects of love this scripture talks about. Gentz says, 'The heart is referred to more than 700 times in the Bible but almost never as a physical organ....One of the most important uses of the term [heart] is to express...total devotion [to God]." When God says that we should love Him with all our heart and soul our souls on my mind, he's talking about loving us him with our intellect,

God's Method

emotions, volition (our will), and our conscience (inner senses).[9] What does each aspect of love mean to you? Look at each aspect separately as it pertains to your walk and ways you can deepen that love personally.

---

[9] Gentz, William H., General Editor, *The Dictionary of Bible and Religion*, Abingdon (Nashville Tennessee, 1986), pg. 431

Chapter 11

It All Depends on You

God's got a plan and God's method will bring us to a place of purpose in Him. And what's more, God doesn't care where you are in life. He loves you with an undying love. He sees you right where you are. He knows your situation. He knows your name. He knows you! He knows you better than you know yourself and He is not alarmed nor distressed concerning our shortcomings, failures and eccentricities.

He's got a plan and a method to meet you right where you are and at the point of your greatest need. He's got a plan and a method that will take you from chaos to order, from inner war---to inner peace.

The enemy's schemes and devices to steal your life, will not succeed. God is the master at methodizing deliverance and victory. God's strategy to bring you into intimate relationship with Him, will work, if YOU work it. When you follow the roadmap, it will lead to you living an overcoming life where victory is the norm. It may be dark now, but there is a light at the end of the road that shines bright. That light will become clearer the more you move towards Him.

He is the supreme organizer, who put a system in place to help facilitate your spiritual victory. He will make you a success, through the power of the Holy Spirit, if you only allow Him entrance into the secret place of your heart and give Him permission to change you.

God's Method

We have got to work with God as He works in us. A victorious spirit-filled life, requires that we walk in agreement with His precepts and in holiness. Jesus says, *"Be ye holy for I am holy"* (I Pet. 1:16). We can't get around His holiness. We can't sidestep His method of sanctification in our lives and expect great victories.

When we cooperate with God's supreme design for our lives, that's when we will see change. We've got to cling to Him. We've got to love Him more than anything or anyone else, even our own lives and ambitions. When we live our lives as a living sacrifice before Him; that's when He will do, what no other power can do.

God's got a method, to sanctify us and to empower us. God's got a method that will confound your enemies and all men will call you blessed. God's got a method that will make your enemies behave and will cause the favor of God to rest upon your life.

God's got a method that will deliver you from poverty and transition you to a place of wealth in body, mind and spirit. God's got a method. It is a method that causes us to live in freedom and to be at peace no matter what winds may blow.

As stated in the introduction, God is a God of order. His plan is to bring us into a healthy and loving relationship with Him as Savior and with others as our spiritual family. He has a plan, that will lead us to a life full of purpose. He has a plan that will allow us to let others know about the God who cares all about them and wants to have relationship with them, too.

God's method is a plan of redemption and holiness. People don't believe in holiness anymore. Anything goes in this society of spiritual relativism and pluralistic worldviews. But, the

Bible says, *"that no man comes unto the Father if he does not accept Jesus Christ as Lord" (John 14:6)*

If we want to know God, we must follow His method for knowing Him, intimately. He has provided a failsafe plan that will work every time, if we work His plan and not our own. There is no reason why we should live on the perimeter of Christianity, teetering on a tightrope, when God has provided life. We must take His plan to heart. God is a God of order. We can shake, dance, shout and sing, but there is still an order that He has set, that will work, if you will apply His precepts to your life and run from clergy clichés, prosperity gospels and heresy, but instead embrace the Logos and his teachings that have endured centuries long. There is no knew formula, only that which is tried and true. Gods ways worked for the early church and it is no different now.

. If we get under God's authority and live in humble obedience to God, we can watch Him work. It doesn't matter what title we hold or our station in life. His method is for every world leader and every street sweeper. It doesn't matter whether we have millions who sit at our feet or whether we are a single parent with a swaddling baby, God desires our single-hearted worship.

When the Israelites were freed from the bondage of Egypt and they were in the desert, they erected a golden calf to worship instead of continuing to worship the God of Moses (Exodus 32). They were a wayward people, who had forsaken their first love and forgotten how God had freed, fed and clothed them. They did not live as a chosen people. They did not live as people of promise because they had traded their position of favor for a false god.

God's Method

Today, God wants us to live as children of the promise and as heirs to His Kingdom. He wants us to live with full access to His love, power and promise. That's why He gave His Son and the Holy Spirit to help us to live with full rights as His children and as His people.

So many of us suffer, when we should have healing. So many live in sorrow, when we should have joy. So many live as weaklings in the Spirit, when we should be strong in the Lord.

Following God's method for a full life gives us access to God and His glory. Many of us want it, but we do not understand His ways. God wants us to know and understand His precepts that gives us full admittance to a complete and victorious life in Christ.

The method set forth herein, is a set of faith and truth that when applied in the life of the believer, leads to a consistent whole for victorious Christian living. These points are not exhaustive. I'm sure that there are those that can add to it, when pondered and meditated upon in the privacy of one's devotional time. This is a foundation from which we can stand, grow and flourish.

While repentance is necessary for entrance to the family of God, it does not stop there. Many have only gone so far as to recite the sinner's prayer for initial conversion. Initiation into the Christian life involves this outward confession of faith and so much more. It is only the beginning of a life journey of faith.

In this day of immediacy in everything that we do, so many neglect the slow and purposeful walk of living with the Christ. We often neglect to allow Him to transform us through His daily method of sanctification.

God still requires the long walk, growing every day, experiencing God in new and fresh ways. This walk is not subject to our own personal beliefs. It is an outline for reaching and experiencing that which is true. It has been said, we can be sincere, but we can also be, sincerely wrong.

When we live the Christian life based on our own catalyst, we are headed for a letdown. God has set the mandate. When we follow and surrender to His precepts, laying aside our preconceived ideas of what ought to be in our own minds, we can experience God in a way that will bring life. We can sort out confusion of what it really means to love Jesus and be a true disciple of Christ.

We were created to glorify God. We were created to adore Him and to have eternal fellowship with God. This is the fulness of the purpose of God. God's method accomplished in our lives will restore that fellowship for it is the means by which union with God is accomplished. The more we get to know God, the more our hearts are stirred towards holy living and we begin to know the purpose of God is for us. God has unique plans and purposes for each person (Psalm 139:13–16), but we can know that, whatever those plans look like, they will ultimately result in our lives bringing glory to Him.

God wants us to know Him deeply. Walking in the Spirit is the vehicle He has provided so we can do so. His Word is truth. To follow His Word, while the world scoffs is what will lead us to the Spirit-filled life.

As the world grows tougher and more combative, the church must return to a place of sanctuary where we exhibit simplicity of love and holiness. As we embrace His method for

God's Method

spiritual fellowship, we will experience the awesome presence of God in our everyday lives which by its very nature is victorious Christian living.

I Corinthians 1:25. "For the foolishness of God is wiser than human wisdom, and the weakness of God is stronger than human strength."

So, abandon doubt and follow His method and experience His presence.

About the Author

Kate Johnson is an ordained minister and has served as a licensed Evangelist in the Church of God in Christ, as well as a Pastor of Outreach and Community Relations for Harvest Outreach Center. As Founder and President of Engage Community Empowerment and Engage Christian Ministers and Psalmists Alliance she serves children, the homeless and seniors in collaboration with other ministries to provide food, clothing and basic, necessities of life.

Katherine holds a Master of Arts in Religion and Christian Thought from Gordon Conwell Theological Seminary. One of her loves is teaching and discipleship. Katherine has served as an adjunct professor teaching New Testament and Early Christian History at Oral Roberts University affiliate school. She has lectured in workshops on worship and women's issues in local churches and conferences. Katherine is not only a preacher, but also a psalmist and published songwriter.

As a writer, she has founded and served as Editor on several newsletters and has penned various articles. Her first book, *On the Brink of Ministry (1997)*, was published under Marimae Publishing, of which she is founder and president and she is a contributing author of the book anthology, *"She Wouldn't Let Me Fall: 100 Stories of Faith Forgiveness & Friendship,"* (2018).

Katherine resides with her husband in Charlotte, N.C. She is a mother and a grandmother and enjoys thrift shopping and estate sales.

God's Method

Book List

Bevere, John, The **Bait of Satan, Living Free from the Deadly Trap of Offense**, Charisma House, Kansas City, MO 2004

Dake, Finis Jennings, **God's Plan for Man**, Dake Publishing, Gainesville, GA (1997)

Dockery, David S. (editor), **Holman Bible Handbook**, Holman Bible Publishers, Nashville, TN 1992

Evans, William, **Great Doctrines of the Bible**, Moody Press, Chicago, IL (1968)

Kendall, R.T., **Total Forgiveness**, Charisma House, Kansas City, MO 2007

Willmington's, Dr. H.L., **Willmington's Guide to the Bible**, Tyndale House, Wheaton IL (1984)

www.ingramcontent.com/pod-product-compliance
Lightning Source LLC
LaVergne TN
LVHW051524070426
835507LV00023B/3285